Trust and Transition

WILEY SERIES
in
STRATEGIC HRM

Series Editor
Neil Anderson

Goldsmiths College, University of London, UK

Competency-based Recruitment and Selection
Robert Wood and Tim Payne

Deception in Selection
Liz Walley and Mike Smith

*Trust and Transition – Managing Today's
Employment Relationship*
Peter Herriot, Wendy Hirsh and Peter Reilly

Further titles in preparation

Trust and Transition
Managing Today's Employment Relationship

Peter Herriot, Wendy Hirsh and Peter Reilly

with Stephen Bevan, Andy Davidson,
Charles Jackson, Polly Kettley, Ivana LaValle,
Adrian Patch, Jo Rick and Penny Tamkin

JOHN WILEY & SONS
Chichester • New York • Weinheim • Brisbane • Singapore • Toronto

        National   01243 779777
        International   +(44) 1243 779777
        e-mail (for order and customer service enquiries): cs-books@wiley.co.uk
        Visit our Home Page on   http://www.wiley.co.uk
                                 or http://www.wiley.com

Other Wiley Editorial Offices

John Wiley & Sons, Inc., 605 Third Avenue,
New York, NY 10158-0012, USA

Weinheim • Brisbane • Singapore • Toronto

Library of Congress Cataloging-in-Publication Data
Herriot, Peter
  Trust and transition : managing today's employment relationship/by
  Peter Herriot, Wendy Hirsh, and Peter Reilly ; with Stephen Bevan . . . [et al.]
  p. cm. — (Wiley series in strategic HRM)
  Includes biographical references and index.
  ISBN 0-471-97929-5 (pbk.)
  1. Manpower planning. 2. Human capital 3. Quality of work life.
  4. Organizational change. I. Hirsh, Wendy. II. Reilly, Peter. III. Bevan, S. (Stephen)
  IV. Title. V. Series: Wiley series in strategic human resource management.
  HF5549.5.M3H475 1998   97–45637
  658.3—dc21   CIP

British Library Cataloguing in Publication Data
A catalogue record for this book is available from the British Library

ISBN 0-471-97929-5

Typeset in Linotype Palatino 10/12pt by Stephen Wright-Bouvier of the
Rainwater Consultancy, Longworth, Oxfordshire.
Printed and bound in Great Britain by Bookcraft (Bath) Limited,
Midsomer Norton, Somerset.
This book is printed on acid-free paper responsibly manufactured from sustainable
forestation, for which at least two trees are planted for each one used.

Editorial Advisory Board

Contents

List of Figures   viii
Series Editor's preface   ix

Part I   Uncharted seas   **1**

Introduction   3
1   Continuity or cataclysm?   11
2   Human resource rhetoric: cost cutting reality   27
3   Personal survival stakes   47
4   Organizational strategy: rational or rationalization?   61
5   Keeping on course   73

Part II   Changing course   **87**

Introduction   89
6   Flexible friends   93
7   Development for transition   109
8   Information exchange: dialogue and transitions   129
9   Managing transitions   147
10 Leadership, trust and transitions   163

Epilogue   179
Index   181

Figures

Figure 1.1   The globalization process   16
Figure 2.1   The vicious circle of cutting costs   38
Figure 4.1   Cycles of change   63
Figure 6.1   Contracting transitions   102
Figure 8.1   Information exchange   131
Figure 9.1   The range of deals   152

Series Editor's preface

Strategic human resource management (HRM) has come of age. Fundamental and core changes in the nature of work and work organization have resulted in far-reaching and universally felt changes in the practice of HRM in industry. Many departments., formerly known under the generic title of 'Personnel Department, have reflected these inescapable changes by renaming the function the 'Human Resource Management Department'. But such changes in name alone do not reflect the more subtle, covert and pervasive themes of change that have afflicted the professional practice of HRM over the last decade or so. HRM has been transformed from being a welfare and administration-oriented service department to a strategically oriented and business policy-setting function which is responsible for much more than the hiring and firing of personnel.

Although the very term HRM has provoked numerous charges of being one of mere empty rhetoric, few would doubt that the demands upon specialist human resource management departments have changed beyond all recognition over more recent years. Flexible forms of working, ad hoc project teams, decentralization, outsourcing of functions and the development of budgets are all factors which have contributed to the coming of age of the HR department. Yet we are far from witnessing the final, logical outcomes to such driving forces for change. Indeed, HR is a function and profession in transition. For this reason, it is important and timely for HR professionals, consultants and practitioners to take stock of the current state of their profession and its concomitant methods, theories and procedures. For while the context within which HR is practised is changing rapidly, some would argue that the profession has struggled to keep pace with these drivers for change, and that simultaneously, while we have seen numerous attempts at innovative practice within HRM, there remains a stable backbone of traditional practice and practices in many industrial sectors.

The tensions within the HR profession have therefore become of paramount concern. Pressures towards cost-effectiveness and ultimatums to demonstrate the real world contribution of HR to any business enterprise do not sit easily alongside more academic treatises on what HR practitioners *should* be doing to stand at the forefront of innovative practice. In fact, some would argue that the practice of HR has become very much more market driven over the last decade, and that the professional status of the HR body has taken second place behind the acute and day-to-day pressures faced by all practising HR managers in their own organizational setting. This second tension, between theory and practice, is one that has arguably led to an increasing divide between researchers and practitioners in HRM. If this has indeed been the case, it is an unfortunate outcome, as each side of the profession can surely learn much from the other. Yet another tension concerns the professional responsibilities and reporting relationships of HR practitioners. Are HR managers primarily members of their own organization's management team, or qualified professionals bringing their own expertise to bear on this particular employing organization? Many practising HR managers will have felt this tension at some point in their careers, and the compelling pressures towards competitive advantage now in both the private and the public sectors of industry have resulted in HR professionals having to demonstrate the 'added value' of their work much more clearly than ever was the case in the past.

Given this changing context for the profession of HRM, the driving forces for business change, and the ambitions and career goals of practising HR managers, it is no surprise that those attempting to practise in the field in the late 1990s face a veritable barrage of conflicting pressures and role requirements. The HR manager has become everything to all employees: a member of the senior management team; a confidant and counsellor for employees; an expert professional belonging to a recognized professional body; facilitator of organizational change; and manager of her or his own HRM department staff, to name but a few of the predominant roles. This lack of role clarity has led undoubtedly to feelings of stress and being a 'Jack of all trades' among many personnel professionals. So where might the way forward lie? Although these conflicting pressures may well have led to role conflict, they have also opened up many doors of opportunity for practising at a strategic level within organizations. Organization development interventions, team building, stress management audits, senior managerial succession planning, employee reward systems, staff appraisal procedures, and contributing to the organization's vision and objectives are all areas which historically were absolute no-go zones for the 'people people' in traditional personnel departments. Yet nowadays, HR professionals are *expected* to make a definite and tangible contribution to many of these areas. It is therefore timely to examine the practice of HR under the title of 'Strategic HRM'.

The objective of the Strategic HRM Series is to bring together cutting edge texts which examine and interpret some of the most pressing concerns for HRM practice in industry. All books in the Series have been written by eminent and acknowledged experts in their own field of practice, whether they happen to be based in academia, consultancy, or industry. Indeed, the authors contributing to the Series do originate from these three different backgrounds. The books attempt to bridge the academic–practitioner divide, but not in a bland matter-of-fact manner, rather, quite the opposite. Authors have been encouraged to be opinionated and to offer a personal commentary on what they as experts in their respective areas believe to be the predominant issues of concern for practising HR managers. Readers should therefore find all texts in the Series thought provoking, carefully considered, but reasoned position statements on the current state of the art of each area addressed by every book in the Series. Books have been written to be easily accessible to the reader, but, nevertheless, to challenge assumptions and traditional practices in HRM. It is my hope, as Series Editor, that every reader will gain something from each book within the Series; that readers will find as much to agree with as to disagree with in each text; but crucially, that all books provide a thought provoking account of changes within the HR profession. Although these house style guidelines have been worked to by all authors contributing to this Series, each volume will nevertheless show an individual style and format which is best suited to the material covered. A stringent editorial policy was therefore intentionally avoided, and indeed, the autonomy to present personal viewpoints, opinions and suggestions for improvement in strategic HRM was encouraged at all stages in the authoring and production process. Books cover a wide range of topics within strategic HRM, and therefore are not intended as 'best practice' how-to texts. Given this diversity of subject matter and approach, it is my hope that the authors have produced texts which will be of interest and concern to practising HR managers. In my view the authors have without exception done a diligent and splendid job in this respect and by so doing have contributed to the debate which promises to shape the future of strategic human resource management in this country.

Neil Anderson
Professor of Work Psychology

PART I

Uncharted seas

Introduction

MARINERS ANCIENT AND MODERN

Joshua Slocum was the first person we know to have sailed round the world on his own. He left Boston in 1895 aged 51, and returned three years later in the sloop he had made with his own hands, the *Spray*. His voyage was a powerful personal experience; in his solitude he felt so lonely that he invented a fellow crew member, and at times even believed in his existence. He faced appalling dangers, but somehow survived and found meaning in his escapes. In his own words:[1]

> One wave, in the evening, larger than others that had threatened all day . . . broke over the sloop fore and aft. It washed over me at the helm, the last that swept over the Spray off Cape Horn. It seemed to wash away old regrets. All my troubles were now astern; summer was ahead; all the world was again before me.

He felt similar oceanic changes as he finally rounded Cape Horn:

> I felt the throb of the great ocean that lay before me. I knew now that I had put a world behind me, and that I was opening out another world ahead.

Yet, despite all his narrow escapes, Slocum succeeded in charting his course across the Pacific so accurately that he arrived within a couple of miles of his destination. As he said:

> I was born in the breezes, and I had studied the sea as perhaps few men have studied it, neglecting all else . . . To know the laws that govern the winds, and to know that you know them, will give you an easy mind on your voyage round the world, otherwise you may tremble at the appearance of every cloud.

When he was not sure what to expect, our hero took the advice of those who did know. The Fuegans, he was warned, were savage marauders who would board the *Spray* at dead of night, slay him and steal his supplies. The way to deal with them was to scatter the deck with tin tacks. They would tread on them with their bare feet, howl in pain and wake Slocum up. He could then fire his gun at them and scare them off. And so it came about, just as he had been advised.

With the aid of some charts, a tin chronometer, a little knowledgeable advice, and his own inestimable knowledge of the sea and seamanship, Joshua Slocum won through. Apart from his courage and endurance, all he needed was know-how. If only that were true today, think personnel professionals and senior managers all over the world. They still need know-how, but it is nowhere near enough. The whole seascape is changing, and the old navigational rules do not always work. In the time it took Slocum to glance at his chronometer, funds can be transferred from London to Tokyo which can destroy an organization or create a new one. In the words of Hamel and Prahalad:[2]

> The first challenge, how to navigate from here to there,
> arises as both public and private institutions struggle
> to plot a course through an increasingly inconstant
> environment, where experience is rapidly devalued
> and familiar landmarks no longer serve as guideposts.
> Never before has the industrial terrain been changing
> so quickly or have industry boundaries been so mal-
> leable . . . How, then, does one get to the future first,
> even when there's no map? How does one invent
> one's own route to the future?

As these authors and many others note, it is next to impossible for organizations to see what their markets, customers, competitors and core skills will be even at the beginning of the next century, let alone in the longer term. How are we to address this uncertainty and navigate a survival course? The answers are not easy, but as we shall show by the end of the book, Joshua Slocum has a lot more to teach us than might at first sight appear.

The sea charts of the management gurus seem to imply the need for the Great Helmsman in the Sky. Organizations, we are told, have to create their future now. Leaders have deliberately to forget most of what they know already and, rather, through vision and foresight, create a picture of a future destination. This may appear unattainable at present. However, it is so attractive to employees that they will be motivated to strive to reach it; they will, in a figure of speech reminiscent of the Spanish Inquisition, be 'stretched and leveraged' not only to dream the impossible dream but also to achieve it.

THE STRATEGIC BUSINESS DILEMMA

'Get real' is the justified response of most people in the hot seat at present to these siren calls. Yes, it is clear that we will need to create or compete for new markets to survive against the competition. Yes, we will have to develop new and better products and services and get them to market more quickly. Yes, we will need new skills and knowledge to enable us to do so. All these things we admit; but they are only half the story.

The other half tells a very different, indeed a contradictory, tale. For the great leap forward advocated by the management gurus, the voyage into uncharted seas with the intent to create a new country, is being required of a crew reduced in numbers and with morale shattered.[3] It is like asking Slocum to set sail round the world when he is convalescing from an attack of scurvy, or whatever it is that old sea dogs suffer from.

The dilemma is acute. **How can we innovate into new markets, services and products when we have destroyed over the last two decades, but especially over the last five years, the conditions necessary to do so?** Innovation needs a willingness to take risks, and therefore a degree of psychological security. It needs a sense of agency and autonomy – the feeling that what you do affects outcomes, and that you can decide what action to take. And while ideas often occur to individuals on their own, teamworking is necessary to bring those ideas through to a finished product, service or system. **Security, agency, autonomy and teamwork** are the conditions for innovation;[4] yet in our desire to cut costs, we have reduced these very conditions to breaking point. By downsizing we have reduced employees' sense of security. By setting tight budget targets and reducing resources we have decreased agency and autonomy, despite all the rhetoric of empowerment. And by concentrating on motivating individuals by performance-related pay, we have shown what little value we place on teamwork.[5]

How are organizations reconciling these two conflicting strategic requirements – to cut costs to the bone and at the same time to innovate? By adopting very different career management strategies for different types of employee. The range of contractual relationships within many of today's organizations is immense:[6] from the so-called zero-hours contract, where workers are not guaranteed any work at all but are expected to turn up when required, through to the careful guidance of a small cadre of potential top managers through a sequence of jobs designed to develop them for the board.

Employers are wanting two sorts of flexibility in order to cut costs. They want flexibility of labour supply – workers working when the need for labour is greatest. And they want flexibility of workers themselves – employees who are prepared to learn and exercise a variety of skills. Different contractual arrangements such as part-time and fixed-term contracts make labour flexibility possible. Their attractiveness to some employees, and the desperation for work of others, make them viable. At the same time, as Atkinson foresaw a dozen years ago,[7] core employees are being promised some degree of security, either in employment or in financial terms, which enhances commitment and encourages innovation. So costs are cut through the varied non-traditional contracts, while innovation is supposedly secured through the better deal being offered to the core.

IS FLEXIBILITY FAILING?

Or so the story goes. Yet we are beginning to doubt whether even these solutions are really being applied strategically. And if they are, whether they are working. The whole employment relationship seems to be fragmenting beyond repair. There used to be a strategic distinction between **developing your own people** so that you can continue to keep a grip on your key markets, and **buying in from outside** so that you can colonize new ones.[8] This has now long gone. Indeed, the aim of embedding a long-term human resources (HR) strategy within a corporate business strategy has become merely aspirational for many.

We are faced instead with the realization that pulling the old motivational strings seems not to be working any more. Even among those to whom we thought we were giving sufficient security to engage their commitment and innovation, we find a marked degree of cynicism and mistrust of top management. The so-called core is crumbling; today it can be just as vulnerable as the periphery when redundancy notices are issued. **Loyalty** and **commitment** are to one's own career, profession or occupation, and immediate colleagues. There is little left for that amorphous entity the organization, and for those distant dictators who run it. And as for those on the wide variety of other contracts, their trust has yet to be earned by fulfilling their terms in spirit as well as in letter and not exploiting them to the organization's short-term advantage.

It is often frustrating for many good organizations: they make contracts with people in good faith, offering training and development and a degree of employment or financial security which it would be hard to match elsewhere. Yet employees' perceptions do not match this reality. They still feel insecure and mistrustful. They have seen what happened in the past to now redundant colleagues, and they have formed their own judgement about the way things are heading.

What is more, they have learned that many of the messages coming down from the top turned out in the end to mean the opposite of what they originally appeared to mean. Instead of delivering on such promises as empowerment or self-development, organizations have been constrained by short-term bottom-line pressures to postpone these aspirations. Furthermore, employees do not believe that organizations are capable of implementing what they promise even should circumstances permit. So both the old implicit career deal of security for loyalty, and also many of the management fads of the last decade, have apparently been reneged upon. Why, then, should employees believe in today's brand new career deals and become good corporate citizens again?

After all, while the idea of career as ladder is outmoded for many, we all need some notion of **career** to make sense of our working life. We need something that ties together and makes sense of our past, our present and our future. We need a story to tell ourselves, if not other people, if we are to be motivated at work. And we need to be confident that we can make a living. What we do not need is to be forced by pressure from above and by job insecurity to work all the hours God sends, putting at risk our health and well-being and catching only occasional glimpses of our nearest and dearest as they grow up or grow old.

Far, therefore, from careers and career management going out of the window along with jobs for life, they are the most important **personnel issue** facing organizations today. For only if careers are successfully managed will organizations have a hope of solving their appalling dilemma of how simultaneously to cut costs and innovate. Yet the current rush to restructure and decentralize, while appearing well suited to address this dilemma, has created as many problems as it has solved. There is a loss of a corporate overview, an absence of cross-fertilization of ideas as the separate businesses and the individual performers strive for their targets. What is more, there are no failsafe mechanisms or spare resources available when processes have been re-engineered and stripped down to their bare bones.

TRUST AND TRANSITION

This book is in two parts. The first part seeks to analyse the employment relationship as a function of the state we are in. We believe that unless we strip away much of the rhetoric that distorts current discussion, we will fail to appreciate the depth of the problems and the complexity of the issues that face us. Hence we will fail to grasp the radical nature of the solutions we need.

In Chapter 1 we will re-examine the familiar old litany of contextual features that are forcing change upon organizations; but this time we will emphasize not only the rapid economic growth but also the loss of much of the **social capital** which is necessary to support it. By social capital we refer to the trust and reciprocity between people that enables them to collaborate. This imbalance between economic growth and social decline, we will argue, implies the need for different approaches to the employment relationship.

Then we will show in Chapter 2 that organizations' current responses tend to decrease further the already diminished social capital available to them. They have lost the trust of their employees. A pervasive insecurity among employees throws further into jeopardy what little trust is still around, as we demonstrate in Chapter 3. This chapter will provide some harder evidence for the general picture we have painted so far. While the objective facts about employment tell a comfortable story for most at present, people do not exude the confidence that the facts appear to justify. On the contrary, the first three chapters demonstrate what happens when the feelings of employees are ignored in the rush to cut costs; or when they are manipulated in search of enhanced commitment and productivity. Trust is lost, and with it the confidence that we can survive in a changing world.

In Chapter 4 we characterize both organizational business change and individual career change as a sequence of **transitions**. Organisations do not pass from one steady state to the next with the greatest of ease; most of them are in a state of constant transition in the effort to maintain some sort of navigational course. Employees likewise: no sooner have they mastered one role than they are moving on to the next. What are the fundamental organizational transitions, and what implications do they have for careers? In Chapter 5 we argue that they are three in number: between growth and contraction; short- and long-termism; and centralization and devolution. These organizational transitions require equally radical career transitions. How can the organization's needs for such radical changes be reconciled with individuals' own needs? Part II, which we will introduce later, gives some different answers.

Joshua Slocum's relationship was with the physical world, a world whose behaviour he could predict and whose territory he could map. The relationship with which personnel professionals are principally concerned, the employment relationship, is social and fluid. Yet even in its present state of flux, we can discern those features which will enable that relationship to survive into the future. They are to be found in the social rules which all relationships require: mutual trust and support in times of transition and change.

REFERENCES

1 Slocum, J. ([1900] 1996) *Sailing Alone Around the World*. London: Orion Books.
2 Hamel, G. and Prahalad, C.K. (1994) *Competing for the Future*. Boston, MS: Harvard Business School Press.
3 Herriot, P. and Pemberton, C. (1995) *New Deals: The Revolution in Managerial Careers*. Chichester: Wiley.
4 West, M. and Altinck, W. (1996) 'Innovation at work: individual, group, organisational, and socio-historical perspectives'. *European Journal of Work and Organisational Psychology* 5 (1): 3–11.
5 Thompson, M. (1992) 'Pay and performance: the employer experience'. Brighton: Institute for Manpower Studies, Report 218.
6 Hirsh, W. and Jackson, C. (1996) 'Strategies for career development: promise, practice, and pretence'. Brighton: Institute for Employment Studies, Report 305.
7 Atkinson, J. (1984) 'Manpower strategies for flexible organisations'. *Personnel Management* 16 (8): 28–31.
8 Cappelli, P. and Crocker-Hefter, A. (1996) 'Distinctive human resources are firms' core competencies'. *Organizational Dynamics* Fall: 7- 23.

Continuity or cataclysm? 1

TRENDS OR TRANSFORMATIONS?

So what is really going on? Is the terrain changing in regular ways so that coastlines are continuously being eaten away? Or is the Bermuda Triangle going to fulfil our worst fears and wreak sudden and untold devastation? Will Slocum's charts continue to serve us well, provided of course that they are continuously updated? Or will we need radically new ways of construing a transformed terrain? In a word, are we talking continuity, or are we talking cataclysm? Should we think in terms of trends, or of transformations?

The continuity camp

Most economists and some management gurus argue for the **continuity** camp. Look, they urge, at the economic and labour market indicators. See the medium-term trends which show clearly that most western economies are in a period of consistent, albeit slow, growth. Observe how this growth has been accompanied by a low rate of inflation, a combination that renders the old boom and bust cycle a mere historical cautionary tale. Or consider productivity. All the figures show that productivity per employee has improved throughout the 1980s and 1990s; why should these trends not continue? Why, oh why, is there so little confidence that they will? And as for employment, here we are in 1998 and the unemployment figures have been going down continuously since 1993. Over the last 20 years, the average length of time spent with an employing organization has decreased by relatively little.[1] Why, then, do people feel so insecure, their foremost worry being that they will lose their job?

Globally, the analysis is the same. The growth rates of different national economies actually differ widely. For some the rate is phenomenal, for others almost static. Population growth demonstrates equally huge differences between nations. Yet the analysis is still in terms of trends rather than in terms of categories or alternative outcomes. The suspicion arises that there is an optimistic view of ultimate growth for all, with differences reflecting different rates of getting there.

Business writers sometimes side with the continuity camp. The old scenario planning techniques which Shell developed after the oil debacle may admittedly no longer be appropriate; two or three models are insufficient to encompass the vast range of possibilities. But, they argue, it is still possible for organizations to ask searching questions about trends; they can still discern the seeds of the future in the trends of the present. The trick is to have a mind open enough to see the possible directions of change. For example:

- How is the trend away from manufacturing and towards service industries likely to affect our current customers' and competitors' business?

- Who has the most to gain and the most to lose?

- To what extent is it possible to modify this change or affect its velocity?

- What does it mean for our current core competencies and those we will need in the future?[2]

There are some trends that we can be completely confident in using for predictive purposes. We know for sure, for example, that the average age of the UK workforce is going to rise over the medium term; we can therefore start addressing some future HR issues before they thrust themselves upon us willy-nilly.

The cataclysmic camp

The opposing camp, the **cataclysmics,** has, paradoxically, a much easier corner to fight. It is not hard to appeal to our desire to see things in black and white terms, even though the challenging new future is portrayed as the opposite of the comfortable old past. The job has died, argues William Bridges;[3] long live 'Me plc'. The old era of coordination and control is over, preaches Tom Peters;[4] chaos not only rules OK but should be actively engineered. We are all post-modernists now, say the social theorists;[5] you can forget the quaint old notion of objective evidence, for it is merely a construction of reality used to maintain elites in power.

These visions of discontinuous change, of apocalypse (or paradise) now, reflect our own ways of making sense of change. Specific events, turning points in our experience, enable us to draw a clear marker between the old and the new. Our relationship with our employer was utterly transformed, we feel in retrospect, when the first compulsory redundancies were announced. There are now two societies in the UK, we believe, not on the basis of the ever-widening objective gap between the rich and the poor, but because yesterday we were mugged. The old order changeth, yielding place to . . . what? We do not know and we do not trust the gurus' visions – but we feel sure it is going to be radically different, and most of us are anxious about our survival in it.

So the professionals are impatient with us for wilfully disregarding the facts as they provide them for our consumption. The gurus of transformation, meanwhile, play upon our fears by talking revolution and casting each of us in the combined role of Robespierre and Lenin.[6] Who is right? Should we, with Slocum, batten down the hatches for the storms we can dimly see ahead? Or should we stop trying to circumnavigate the world and build a prototype spaceship instead? Do the canons of navigation still apply, or must we invent new rules of the game?

Of course, what we are really dealing with here are two different perspectives. The economists' view deals in **quantifiable abstractions**: gross domestic product, rate of inflation, average labour cost per working hour, etc. Inevitably we think in terms of trends when faced with evidence that these variables show consistent change over time. What is more, because of the status of economists, we accept not only their measurements as correct, but also their assumption that these are the variables with which we should concern ourselves. But their measures may vary according to how they are calculated or presented: witness UK unemployment figures. And their choice of which variables to measure depends upon their assumptions about what is important. Nevertheless, we give them due respect and treat their data as 'objective'. The feelgood factor, in contrast, despite the best efforts of pollsters and social scientists, can never attain the same scientific respectability. It is the economic indicators that win out when business people try to understand change and adapt to it.

Yet it is the subjective view that usually dominates in the end. For example, despite an economy behaving virtuously on nearly all the indicators, the Labour Party won the UK 1997 election with a landslide. And we are far more likely to construe our personal experience in categorical terms. Categories and classes of people and events, rather than disembodied graphs or trends, are our usual way of making sense of the world.[7] And it is even better when the categories are binary: old or new, employment or unemployment, secure or insecure, fair or unfair, etc. It is all too easy to dismiss people's interpretation of their experience as mere perception, and usually faulty perception at that; after all, we sneer, look at what the data show. Yet to ignore or belittle such perceptions is doubly dangerous. The obvious danger is that people's behaviour is guided more by their own perceptions than by economists' graphs. The less obvious one is that we pay little attention to the content of people's concerns, what it is that really worries them.

Those concerns are as much about **social** as **economic** issues; they relate to the institutions which support people's lives and the social relationships which sustain them. In the brave new world of the global economy, we only attend to such social issues when they offer a threat to growth. Visions of a revolting underclass give the occasional moment's pause to the rush for competitive advantage at all costs.[8] Yet in fact any sustainable future depends as much upon social as it does upon financial capital.

We will argue in this chapter that while global economic capital is growing, social capital, the very basis of collaboration and trust, is diminishing. Since an adequate level of social capital is a necessary condition for economic growth, the global project will fail unless nations and organizations take urgent steps to replenish their social capital. This requirement will dominate the employment relationship of the future.

ECONOMIC CHANGE:
THE GENIE FROM THE GLOBAL BOTTLE

Changes in economic capital are staggering in their speed and intensity. Their drivers are well known; every business book goes through the same list, differing only in the importance they attach to each.[9][10] Technological change, deregulation, competition, and globalization always feature. However, the way in which each of these drivers interacts with the others, so that the effect is multiplicative rather than additive, is not always brought out so clearly. We will attempt briefly to do so now.

The global level

Globally, economic and political liberalization have opened up new national markets for exploration and competition. At the same time, however, these new markets themselves rapidly become competitors. Moreover, deregulation within national economies has enabled organizations to enter markets that were previously reserved to specific organizations or occupations alone. Thus at the global level we see such countries as China, that have recently been opened up as markets, already starting to compete effectively. The story of the eastern Tiger economies is by now well known.[11] At the national level, a whole new set of players has emerged, to compete for what are usually relatively static markets. The market for financial services in the UK, for example, is now served by a wide variety of organizations, and the consequent fallout in this sector is only just beginning.

As nations emerge into the global market, they rapidly acquire the investment in knowledge, skills and technology to enable them to compete successfully with mature economies that have higher labour costs. Such investment usually originates from these self-same mature economies, since a higher return on capital is forecast from the emerging nations.

Information technology helps in two fundamental ways. It enables capital to be transferred in an instant; and it permits knowledge to be transferred relatively quickly. Hence inward investment and urgent educational expansion have created national competitors where only markets used to be. Figure 1.1 summarizes this process overall.

The organizational level

At the organizational as well as at the global and national levels the same processes are at work. Given the transferability of work in place and time, transnational organizations get their work done where it is cheapest to do so.[12] We are familiar with routine word-processing activities being located in developing countries. Now, software and design engineering and the auditing of accounts can be carried out in India rather than in the western nation where the organization was probably born. There is thus an increasing level of cost competition, particularly for organizations located primarily in relatively high-wage economies. At the same time, these organizations in western nations are forced to innovate and bring better goods and services, tailored to customers' needs, to market more quickly. Otherwise they will fail to add the value necessary to compensate for the lower costs of their new rivals.

The national level

This is why both nationally and at the organizational level, the UK, like several other European nations, is faced with the dilemma to which we referred in the Introduction: how to bear down on costs and simultaneously innovate into new markets. Nationally, we seem to have decided that the country is better off seeking to compete on cost alone. We have welcomed inward investment to the UK based upon deregulated low-wage manufacturing assembly; meanwhile foreign companies take over

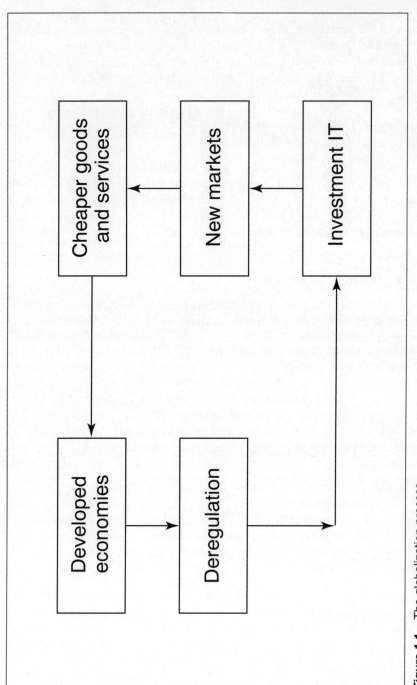

Figure 1.1   The globalization process

many of the remaining large manufacturers, locating research and development (R&D) elsewhere. UK organizations suffer further handicaps relative to their foreign competitors. They are under constant pressure to improve shareholder dividends regularly.[13] If they fail to do so, they will be written down by the financial analysts of the City of London and become targets for takeover bids. Hence it is hardly surprising that more short-term competitive effort has been put into cost reduction than into investment in innovation in the longer term.

There have also been several well-documented trends in the UK economy. These are:

- from manufacturing to service sectors
- from large to medium and small organizations
- from manual to managerial, professional, and technical occupations.

There have also been several radical responses by organizations which we will review in the next chapter. However, what we are primarily concerned to do here is to note the sheer complexity, speed and scale of current economic change. There is no reason to suppose that these features will not characterize the next millennium too. Hence the pressure on global, national and organizational social capital to cope with the implications of economic change will be immense. Have we sufficient reserves in the societal bank to cope? If not, where can we generate more?

THE SOCIAL TORTOISE AND THE ECONOMIC HARE

As usual, the extravert economic hare hogs the limelight. Fast, hot and sexy he dominates the business press and the gurus' best sellers. Yet, devalued and slow moving though he is, the social tortoise provides the bedrock without which the hare sinks and drowns in the sea of mud upon the track. All the attention is focused on the hare, yet it is the tortoise that decides the outcome.

Social capital

We argue that many of the difficulties faced today by nations and by organizations are the result of wilfully ignoring the importance of social capital. For the last two decades, we have concentrated upon *homo oeco-*

nomicus, human beings as rational optimizers of their own benefits. We have largely ignored *homo socius*, human beings as people who have to relate to one another in order to survive. Indeed, we were told by teacher at one point that 'there is no such thing as society'.

On the contrary, it is only when economic and social capital are considered together that a workable synthesis for the future can emerge. This synthesis at the organizational level of analysis consists of new rules for the employment relationship and the management of careers.

Social capital represents the fund of trust and goodwill in any social group that enables people within it to collaborate with each other without having to first write a legal agreement 20 pages long. It is thus fundamental to organizational success. If you cannot trust others to fulfil their side of the bargain, you are only going to commit yourself to action if you are guaranteed recompense in the event of the other reneging on their obligations. This results in insupportable transaction costs[14] and vast fortunes to lawyers. Social capital is based on the notion of reciprocity; the social norm of fulfilling mutual obligations. Strictly speaking, trust increases as obligations continue to be met.

In a masterly account, Francis Fukuyama[15] demonstrates the truth of two fundamental propositions: first, at the very least, a high level of national social capital and national economic success are closely related – the greater a nation's social capital, the more likely it is to enjoy economic growth. Of course, the direction of causality is crucial; it is much easier to fulfil obligations when you can afford to do so, we may argue. But Fukuyama shows clearly that nations with comparable natural resources differ markedly in their social capital and growth rates.

Second, social capital can be created through a wide variety of social institutions. While Italy and China derive theirs primarily from strong family units, Germany has historically had powerful local government structures, and Americans form clubs for just about anything and also attend church in large numbers. The origin of a nation's social capital affects the nature of organizations; so there are myriad small and medium-sized family businesses in Italy and China in such sectors as clothing and fashion and services. The broader scale of social institutions in Germany and Japan results in excellence in larger scale enterprises in different sectors, especially manufacturing.

Social change

While economic capital is still growing, albeit at a reduced rate, social capital is slowly dissipating. Slowly, that is, in comparison with the rate of economic change, but certainly not slowly compared to historic rates of social change. Social change is by its very nature far slower than economic change. For fundamental social change requires changes in cultures, and cultures are notorious for their tenacity. To change a culture requires changes not only in value priorities but also in basic beliefs about the nature of the physical and social world.[16] Optimists who have engaged in national and organizational culture change programmes have discovered this tenacity to their cost. The Chinese family survived the Cultural Revolution, and professionals in the National Health Service still retain the unfashionable belief that clinical criteria are more important than those of cost.

TRUST BUST: THE DESTRUCTION OF SOCIAL CAPITAL

The statement that social capital is being dissipated faster than it can be created is certainly true of the developed western world, and may well apply globally too. In global terms, we have squandered the social capital derived from transnational organizations such as the United Nations and the World Bank. The high hopes of the post-war settlement have given way to the dominance of national over international interests, to the extent that the necessary financial support for effective collaborative action is not forthcoming.

   Government itself has become a dirty word; indeed, to diminish the role of government has become an election manifesto promise across the world. Government is no longer seen as an institution whose function is to ensure social benefits such as peace, security and justice for its citizens; in some countries it is not even seen as a necessary constraint upon individual liberty. Rather, it is sometimes portrayed as a worldwide conspiracy to take people's freedom away from them. Taxes are viewed not as a way of redistributing resources so that all may share in national prosperity to the extent of receiving the necessities of life; rather, they are an imposition upon those who deserve to keep all they have succeeded in acquiring. Moreover, economic growth and employment have become decoupled; it no longer sounds strange to announce increases in profits and multiple redundancies in the same annual company report. On the contrary, the redundancies are paraded as achievements. In the words of J.K. Galbraith,[17] we live in a 'Culture of Contentment'. The comfortable majority is wilfully ignoring the fact that its way of life is fast destroying the social capital upon which it ultimately depends.

Potential sources of social capital

New social institutions are emerging, and some old ones are returning with renewed vigour. Will they replenish the fund of social capital necessary to support economic growth? It seems doubtful that they will. We are seeing a resurgence of **nationalism** as empires break up and long-repressed differences between civilizations become the badges of new or resurrected nationhood.[18] Meanwhile, isolationist and xenophobic political parties are gaining ground in many developed nations. Religious **fundamentalism**, likewise, is speading apace. Both these developments usually result in very strong reciprocity and shared identity inside the national or religious group, but hostile attitudes to those outside them. Business and other working relationships will therefore be very difficult with outsiders, yet the global economy demands that such relationships be successful.

A similar development in the industrialized and post-industrialized nations is the growth of **issuism**. Those for whom a single issue is their major preoccupation have little time for those whose horizons are broader. In the cases of religious fundamentalism and issuism, it is unlikely that the world of work features high in their priorities; the oft-quoted relationship of the Protestant Reformation and the Industrial Revolution is an example not so much of religious fundamentalism as of cultural revolution. And as for nationalism, economic growth is rarely its first concern.

We can discern some other developments which perhaps hold greater promise of enhancing our stock of social capital. **Regionalism**, for example, often draws upon a common cultural identity to enable interdependent industrial sectors to collaborate within a nation state or across national boundaries.[19] Lombardia and Catalonia are European examples, and Hong Kong with Shenzhen Province is an Asian one. Local culture allied to inter-sector and inter-organizational collaboration, supported by a shared infrastructure, provides a strong basis for reciprocity at work.

A second potential source of social capital for the future is **professionalism**. The membership of a professional group creates a common language and interests which transcend national and organizational boundaries. In contrast to this, professions can be seen as exclusive attempts to colonize various occupational territories, so collaboration with other professions may not be so easy.[20]

Finally, we can discern the emergence of various **global concerns** where issues of the survival of the human race transcend all other interests. Issues such as the environment, health and peace have the potential to generate global social capital, but they are way down the agenda of most countries, especially those currently enjoying rapid economic growth.

The national picture

National pictures are microcosms of this global scenario. In the UK, for example, we have increased the gap between the richest and the poorest 10 percents of the population such that the income of the richest has increased by 63 percent in real terms over the past 13 years, while the poorest have suffered a decrease of 17 percent.[21] Other nations show a similar increasing gulf between rich and poor, with New Zealand among the leaders. Many of our social institutions which have historically been our source of social capital are in decay or are disintegrating before our very eyes. Parliament, the church, the monarchy, the law, the National Health Service, schools, the BBC and press, local government, the police, and the family itself are all for one reason or another decreasing in their capacity to provide social capital. Some of these institutions have failed to adapt to people's changing needs, others have been deliberately targeted by government, and others again have lacked the support and resources necessary to fulfil their functions. Often two or all three of these reasons apply. Overall the result is clear: the old sources of reciprocity and trust are diminished, together with their ideological justification. People have less opportunity to learn to trust one another.

Furthermore, we have lost much of the trust we learned when we were younger. Middle-aged and older people perceive the **social contract** with the state to which they thought they had signed up as having been reneged upon.[22] Lives were built around contributions from personal income to the state, for which one received pension, insurance, healthcare and education for one's children. It is all very well, people feel, to say that adequate provision cannot now be made from the public purse for these necessities, but it is a bit rich to apply this decision retrospectively.

Just as many perceive their social contract with the state to have been broken, so they feel that their **psychological contract**[23] with their employer has likewise been consigned to the dustbin of history. In an often unspoken deal, they traded their loyalty, conformity and skills in exchange for job security, wage increases and the prospect of promotion. While working people may not have enjoyed all the features of this managerial and professional contract, at least they had a degree of security won for them by their unions. The feeling of betrayal and the loss of trust have been exacerbated by the perceived inequity in the fortunes of top management. These have received far greater rises in rewards in percentage terms than everyone else, and such rises have borne little relationship to the organizational performance to which they were supposedly linked. Even when they too are made redundant, top people's golden handshakes are grotesquely disproportionate.

We are not arguing that the old social or psychological contracts are nationally or organizationally sustainable in the present economic climate. We cannot go back to the old deals. What we do maintain is that many now feel that they have been cheated, and that they can trust neither government nor employer to keep any promise or obligation in the future.[24] The advocates of 'Me plc' are therefore tapping a rich vein of cynicism and individualism. Older people have acquired these characteristics painfully; the young are familiar with them as daily facts of life.

Individual as hero

The economists' view of people as rational individuals, taking decisions solely on the basis of the balance of individual costs and benefits, has dominated political and economic discourse until recently in the USA and the UK. Rewards have been allocated on the basis of individual performance, and individual accountability for bottom-line targets has been stressed. Organizational success has been consistently attributed to the efforts of individuals, and a sequence of organizational heroes has dominated the management literature since the 1960s. Gurus and consultants have been obsessed with discovering the ultimate individual heroes who can lead organizations into the promised land.

In the 1960s and 1970s, the chief executives of the big US companies were the corporate heroes. In the 1980s, the frontline worker at the sharp end assumed the heroic mantle when the CEOs turned out to have feet of clay. Now we have new heroes, the 'Real Change Leaders'.[25] These are a new breed of middle manager:

> who lead initiatives that influence dozens to hundreds
> of others to perform differently – and better – by
> applying multiple leadership and change approaches.

These Archangel Gabriels not only take continuous risks with their career prospects by harrying top management and bypassing procedures. They also say oleaginous things such as:

> it was one of those times when I had to reach deep
> inside and remind myself that I have been overwhel-
> med before and that somehow it can be done.

The collective perspective

Yet the economic challenges and changes that we are facing actually require us to take a collective rather than an individualistic perspective:

- We will need to operate internationally more and more, learning to collaborate effectively with people of national cultures different from our own.[26] [27]

- We will have to work together with people from organizations with which we have an alliance (e.g. British Petroleum and Mobil) or a customer or supplier relationship (e.g. Marks and Spencer and its suppliers).[28]

- As the environment changes ever more rapidly, mutual commitment and trust among colleagues and between top management and the rest becomes more vital if the organization is to adapt in time and so survive.

- If new products and services require multidisciplinary teams to develop them and get them more quickly to market, then people with different perspectives and different skill sets will need to work effectively together.

- If the diversity of the customer base is to be matched by an equivalent organizational diversity, then more cooperation between people with different backgrounds and assumptions will be required.

- And finally, and perhaps most important of all, if employees are expected to 'delight the customer', if they are to go the extra mile and be good organizational citizens,[29] then they have to believe that the organization will do the same for them when they need it. This sort of trust is not just the basic belief that the other party will fulfil their side of the bargain; it is also the expectation that they will, out of a mixture of altruism and self-interest, go beyond it.

The conclusion is inescapable. If the economic and business changes which we are facing require an increasing degree of trust, and if the fund of social capital derived from civil society is decreasing, then organizations will have to create their own social capital. They cannot rely on employees to bring much with them when they join.

Yet increasing trust will alone not be enough. As we will argue, it is a necessary, but not sufficient condition for organizational survival. Trust is needed in order to support **transition**.

Some questions to think about

1. What is your own view of the nature of change in your organization: do you perceive it as continuous or cataclysmic? How does the view you hold affect the way you manage? What do you think is the prevalent perception of change in your organization: a one-off upheaval? a series of upheavals? continuous and reasonably predictable? continuous and unpredictable? What effects have these perceptions had on staff motivation and morale?

2. Do you have an overall picture of how globalization, deregulation, enhanced competition and technology are interacting to affect your national economy, your business sector and your organization? How might/does such an overview influence your decisions?

3. The trends from manufacturing to service, from large organizations to SMEs and from manual to technical/managerial/professional work are now well established. Have you worked out their implications for your organizational direction and for your personnel policies and practices?

4. If you believe that the fund of social capital has decreased, in what ways has your organization suffered as a consequence of such a decrease? To what extent have these deleterious consequences been made worse by the concentration upon individuals and their performance typical of many western cultures?

REFERENCES

1 Gregg, P. and Wadsworth, J. (1996) 'A short history of labour turnover, job tenure, and job security, 1975–1993'. *Oxford Review of Economic Policy* 11 (1): 73–90.
2 Hamel, G. and Prahalad, C.K. (1994) *Competing for the Future*. Boston, MS: Harvard Business School Press.
3 Bridges, W. (1995) *Jobshift: How to Prosper in a Workplace without Jobs*. London: Nicholas Brealey.
4 Peters, T. (1992) *Liberation Management: Necessary Disorganization for the Nanosecond Nineties*. New York: Alfred A. Knopf.
5 Wakefield, N. (1990) *Postmodernism: The Twilight of the Real*. London: Pluto.
6 Senge, P.M. (1990) *The Fifth Discipline: The Art and Practice of the Learning Organization*. New York: Doubleday.
7 Hampson, S.E. (1982) *The Construction of Personality*. London: Routledge and Kegan Paul.

8 Galbraith, J.K. (1992) *The Culture of Contentment*. New York: Houghton Mifflin.
9 Hamel, G. and Prahalad, C.K. (1994) *Competing for the Future*. Boston, MS: Harvard Business School Press.
10 Porter, M.E. (1990) *The Competitive Advantage of Nations*. New York: Free Press.
11 Ohmae, K. (1985) *Triad Power*. New York: Free Press.
12 Bartlett, C. and Ghoshal, S. (1989) *Managing across Borders: The Transnational Solution*. Boston, MS: Harvard University Press.
13 Hutton, W. (1994) *The State We're In*. London: Jonathan Cape.
14 Williamson, O.E. (1993) *The Nature of the Firm: Origins, Evolution, and Development*. Oxford: Oxford University Press.
15 Fukuyama, F. (1995) *Trust: The Social Virtues and the Creation of Prosperity*. New York: Free Press.
16 Schein, E.H. (1985) *Organizational Culture and Leadership*. San Francisco: Jossey Bass.
17 Galbraith, J.K. (1992) *The Culture of Contentment*. New York: Houghton Mifflin.
18 Huntington, S.P. (1996) *The Clash of Civilizations and the Remaking of World Order*. New York: Simon & Schuster.
19 Ohmae, K. (1995) *The End of the Nation State*. New York: Free Press.
20 Abbott, A. (1988) *The System of Professions: An Essay on the Division of Expert Labour*. Chicago: University of Chicago Press.
21 Social Justice Commission (1994) *Social Justice: Strategies for National Renewal*. London.
22 Hutton, W. (1994) *The State We're In*. London: Jonathan Cape.
23 Rousseau, D.M. (1995) *Psychological Contracts in Organizations*. California: Sage.
24 Robinson, S.L. and Rousseau, D.M. (1994) 'Violating the psychological contract: not the exception but the norm.' *Journal of Organizational Behaviour* 15, 245–59.
25 Katzenbach, J. (1995) *Real Change Leaders*. New York: McKinsey & Co.
26 Hofstede, G. (1980) *Culture's Consequences*. London: Sage.
27 Trompenaars, F. (1993) *Riding the Waves of Culture*. London: Nicholas Brealey.
28 Kanter, R.M. (1989) *When Giants Learn to Dance*. New York: Simon and Schuster.
29 Organ, D.W. (1990) 'The motivational basis of organizational citizenship behavior', in B.M. Staw and L.L. Cummings (eds) *Research in Organizational Behavior*, vol. 12. Greenwich, CT: JAI Press.

Human resource rhetoric: cost cutting reality

2

THE RATIONAL BUSINESS RESPONSE

Faced with the demands of the new business and economic context, most western organizations have understandably put all their time and effort into adapting to it. They have striven to ensure their survival, and maybe even their growth. They have adopted a wide variety of ideas, structures, and systems, and sought to obtain employees' commitment to them. But they have not been aware of the importance of social capital, nor of its loss in civil society and therefore of its decrease within the organizational context. The consequence has been that instead of enhancing the organization's stock of social capital before embarking on radical change, top management has inadvertently decreased that stock still further.

Ideas, and tools to put them into practice, have been ten a penny. Many of them have admirably addressed the issues that the business context has raised. Organizations have been urged to face outward rather than inward, to turn towards the customer rather than to contemplate the beauty of their existing structures and systems. Only by focusing externally will organizations create and exploit the new global markets and compete adequately for their share of the old ones.

Strategic requirements

In order to compete with nations and companies which can produce goods and provide services cheaper, western organizations have sought to add value to the customer by superlative quality and by tailoring to the needs of individuals. Consumerism demands nothing less. Hence employees have to be capable of learning new skills and knowledge, so as to develop or provide these new products and services. They have to be flexible people, willing to change what it is they offer, and capable of adapting to the requirements of customers.

In order to meet the needs of the customer and respond quickly to them, those who deal face to face with customers and clients need to be able to take decisions themselves. Apart from the personal skills required to solve problems and come up with creative solutions, employees need to be free from bureaucratic controls in order to satisfy customers individually and quickly. Hence it is appropriate to remove the layers of middle management to which they used to refer such decisions. This can be seen structurally as flattening the pyramid within a business, and processually as devolving authority from a corporate centre to autonomous business units.

Given the removal of levels of control and the consequent increase in the traditional span of managerial control, different ways of managing people's performance are clearly needed, since they are now to be more autonomous in their day-to-day work than hitherto. And in order to provide a clear framework of guiding principles and values within which employees are free to take their own decisions, leadership is required to give meaning, purpose and inspiration.

To help achieve these aims, a wide variety of tools and systems has been developed. A recent piece of research[1] found that British companies simultaneously used an average of eleven management tools, including total quality management, performance-related pay, mission and vision statements, self-directed teams and so on. While these tools were marketed with much hype, and although their unintended results were often damaging, nevertheless they bore some sort of rational relationship to the ideas of quality and innovation which they were designed to support.

The human resources function

The human resources (HR) function was allocated a central role in this scenario – to support the business by utilizing to the full the capacities of the employees in the achievement of business objectives. Since success depended so obviously on employees, HR's ability to foster quality and innovation was considered crucial. Yet, as we will argue, the actions which HR had to take in helping to cut costs, and the justifying rhetoric to which it subsequently subscribed, soon removed its credibility. Sometimes branded as top management's stooges, its much-coveted seat at top table rendered it irretrievably upstairs rather than halfway up, on the landing.

Yet the appearance of power often masked HR's real impotence. Frequently not consulted when the consultants sold the next fad to the CEO, it was saddled with trying to ensure implementation by an unwilling workforce. And while having an input to business decisions is gratifying, it is not so pleasing to manage the human consequences of the cost cutting to which you have been a party.

Cost cutting

Innovation, quality and added value were not the only strategic requirements. There was also the prior one of cutting costs. Particularly in the
context of the expectations of investors, but also in the light of lower
labour costs elsewhere, cost competitiveness was a necessary condition
for survival. It was not likely to be sufficient for long-term growth, but it
was an immediate imperative for most.

The driving concepts here were:

- reducing labour costs, the quickest way of making large-scale savings
- flexible use of labour so peaks of demand could be met while costs
  were saved in the troughs
- increasing productivity per worker to reduce the cost of unit of output
- outsourcing all non-core activities so as to remove all possible permanent employment costs
- acquiring or disposing of businesses in order to achieve economies of
  scale or to be rid of any part of the organization which did not add
  value.

Again, a wide range of tools and systems was developed to achieve these
ends. Business process re-engineering, for example, is aimed at reducing
cost and improving productivity by redesigning in as simple a way as
possible the organization's fundamental business processes. A bewildering variety of employment contracts is now on offer in order to achieve
labour flexibility. And a whole new industry of outplacement consultants
has developed as a way of seeking to manage redundancies in a humane
way.

Management of strategic requirements

Unfortunately, the two strategic objectives, cutting costs and innovating,
are mutually incompatible unless they are managed with consummate
skill and in the context of mutual trust between top management and
others. Otherwise the obvious contradictions resulting from putting cost

cutting first and then demanding innovation are fatal. For example:

- How can employees be empowered to take decisions, when they have insufficient resources to carry through those decisions?

- How can staff provide a super-quality service, when there are insufficient people to provide it and when the most experienced have been sacked?

- How can people devote time to learning and self-development, when the pressures of performance and productivity targets bear down daily upon them?

- How can organizations learn, when they have outsourced major parts of the value chain?

- How can leaders inspire and provide meaning, when they are held responsible by the workforce for redundancies and corporate failures?

- How can middle managers cope with the conflicting requirements to cut costs and at the same time to help people develop, empower them etc.?

KEY POINT

A public sector technical organization, now an agency, recently looked at the skill needs of its engineering staff, most of whom have a craft engineering background. Cost pressures have driven down the training capability of the organization in spite of the fact that it has to compete on quality and speed as well as on cost. Keeping a balance between cost containment and investment in the skills of the workforce will be the key factor in whether the organization survives.

INNOVATION AND QUALITY FALL BEHIND

The evidence demonstrates the difficulties organizations have experienced in reconciling the cutting of costs with the encouragement of innovation and quality. If the rolling out of a carefully integrated sequence of measures in which the systems for dealing with employees were aligned with one another and with the business plans is an indication of such reconciliation, then the two strategic aims could not be further apart. For the general story is one of piecemeal implementation,[2] in which any attempt to enhance innovation is immediately followed by yet another cost-cutting measure.

Human resource management

Of course the idealized picture of strategy rationally derived and rolled out is a prescriptive management myth. As two of the most prominent HR research groups in the UK have clearly demonstrated, human resource management policies and practices occur when the conditions favour their implementation. Human resource management policies are, broadly speaking, those described at the beginning of this chapter, aimed at making a strategic response to environmental changes, but not dominated by the need to cut costs. It is in organizations with a complex but coherent set of products or services (and a correspondingly complex organizational structure) that these ideas, policies and practices are more likely to occur.[3] And while top management's visible commitment and support is necessary, it is certainly not sufficient: employee involvement, and maybe union and governmental support, are also required.[4]

An interesting further contradiction is this: the existence of a central HR function is associated with coherent HR policies and practices.[5] Yet in many organizations keen to devolve decision-making down the line, line managers and business units have taken over the HR responsibilities that corporate HR used to hold. Even the most traditionally centralized organizations such as the big retail banks have moved in this direction. Perhaps this is why opportunism reigns supreme in diversified conglomerates, while a degree of coherence is only to be found in more unified organizations.[6] Overall, though, we have to ask: has the HR function dared to question top management's desire to commoditize people in the way that the posh new 'Human Resources' label implies?

Wherever cost competition is intense, however, those interventions aimed at treating employees as costs to be minimized and as commodities to be maximally utilized will prevail.[7] This will effectively negate the effects of any policies or practices designed to enhance innovation and quality or to add value. It is when we look at the evidence about individual practices that the malign consequences of attempts to enhance productivity and cut costs at the same time become more apparent.

Performance-related pay

Consider performance management, and in particular, one element of performance management, performance-related pay (PRP). PRP's intended outcomes are an increase in motivation, reward for contribution rather than for seniority, and hence a perception of greater equity and a clear message about what is valued. By the early 1990s, most UK organizations were practising it.[8] Yet the proportion of PRP to total pay was only 4 per cent in 1991,[9] and most of the money was paid to higher graded staff. There were many occasions when a local unit and individuals within it achieved the targets for which bonuses were payable, but these were withheld on the basis of poor overall financial performance at the business or corporate level. Or else, a fixed pot of money had already been allocated to PRP, regardless of final performance figures. Furthermore, few organizations spent enough time or money on training line managers to assess performance and conduct performance reviews, on communicating the process and objectives, and on involving staff on the design side.[10] Hence, because of the need to cut costs, any potential benefits of PRP have largely been lost. Instead the main concern of staff is with the inequity of the small allocations that are made.

Total quality management

A look at total quality management (TQM) shows the bases to be:

- to conform to the requirements of the customer, where 'customers' include others in one's own organization as well as those traditionally so called

- benchmarking and statistical process control to ensure performance is monitored and immediately corrected

- involvement and commitment of all to the aim of supplying zero-defect goods or services

- a continuous improvement towards these ends and towards the elimination of any sort of waste.

Unfortunately, most organizations appeared to be unwilling to devote the resources necessary to achieve these long-term aims. Rather, they treated TQM as a quick-fix bolt-on extra to boost short-term performance and reduce the costs of faulty product.[11] [12] Hence the expected benefits have failed to emerge for most companies which embraced the concept and its tools, and their explicit use is now declining.

Training and development

Finally, look at training and development, surely the key to an innovative and flexible workforce. According to the Labour Force Survey,[13] the percentage of those of working age in Great Britain who had received

---

The case of graduates: segmentation in action

A follow-up study of former students of the University of Sussex who had graduated between 1991 and 1993 demonstrated that:

- only a quarter moved straight into a permanent job, in which they then stayed for a further three years
- a third was employed on fixed-term contracts, almost half of which were less than a year in duration
- 6 percent were self-employed
- 40 percent were in small firms (under 200 employees)
- in the end, however, most found full-time employment (Connor and Pollard[16]).

Why is the job situation of graduates so varied?

- Over two-thirds are graduating with debts of between £3000 and £10, 000.
- As a consequence, they take the first, often low-paid job which they are offered.
- Employers focus their recruiting efforts on Oxbridge and the older universities.

Cost cutting leads to segmentation everywhere, including among those upon whose development a lot of money has already been invested (Purcell and Pitcher[17]).

job-related training in the previous four weeks rose steadily during the boom years of the late 1980s to reach a peak in 1990. It then reduced during the recession. More recent evidence[14] indicates that:

- Much of the effort and resources in training and development is being put into senior managers and high potential staff. Some of these still have a planned organizational career in the traditional sense.

- Professionals and technical workers, however, have to strike deals with their employer in order to assure themselves of the possibility of developing.

- The rest of the workforce is expected to engage in 'self-development' in order to be able to contribute more, but the degree of support for such learning activities varies considerably.[15]

- For some, training is solely to improve their performance at their present job – to make them more efficient.

To the extent that training and development for all staff is fundamental to improved quality and added value then, this segmentation of provision within the same company is unlikely to benefit the organization as a whole. Rather, it will increase cynicism and perceptions of inequity.

All of these three areas of HR policy and practice, performance-related pay, total quality management, and training and development have not had the results that were expected. In part, this may be because they were wrongly conceived; individual PRP, for example, militates against the teamworking necessary for quicker innovation to market. But top management's unwillingness to commit the necessary resources to them as a consequence of the prior need to cut costs must bear most of the responsibility.

COST CUTTING SURGES AHEAD

When we turn to methods for cutting costs and enhancing productivity, however, we find a different story, although often a somewhat confused one.

Downsizing

First, consider downsizing, that is, making people redundant. The press headlines announce repeated waves of redundancies in large organizations, especially the recently privatized utilities. British Telecom, for example, decreased in size from 245,000 employees in 1990 to 134,000 in 1996, despite record profits. Yet some organizations are making senior people redundant while recruiting vigorously at younger and lower levels. In 1992, 35 percent of organizations claimed that more managers were employed than five years previously.[18] Overall, job losses have been greater recently in larger organizations, especially those in the utilities, retail and government sectors.

Given the difficulties of getting reliable information from organizations themselves, the best data are obtained from more general labour market statistics. The Labour Force Survey, for example, shows that in spring 1989 around 140,000 people had been made redundant within the last three months, whereas in spring 1991, the figure was nearly 400,000.[19] Again, as with training and development, these data demonstrate the need to cut costs in recession rather than a strategic restructuring.

The picture overall is nevertheless of many employees enjoying long tenure with one employer; for example, around 50 percent of those in the working age population in 1993 had over five years tenure, and 30 percent had more than ten years.[20] However, the number of full-time jobs to which a full-time worker who had recently been made redundant might aspire is decreasing apace.

Flexible contracts

Which brings us on to our next method of cutting labour costs: flexible contracts. Managers themselves agree that the need to reduce costs is the key factor motivating their decisions on the shape and size of the workforce.[21] This is the fourth year running that they have said this. Increased flexibility of contract enables them to match labour availability to demand more efficiently. It also saves certain employment costs which legally apply only to full-time 'permanent' staff. Almost 90 percent of respondents reported that their organizations used part-time and temporary workers in 1995, a 10–15 percent rise on 1994. Only 47 percent estimated that in four years' time they would still be employing 90 percent and more of their workers on full-time contracts, while 45 percent said that they would be employing only 75 percent and more full-timers.

Of course, we need to take these statements of intent with a pinch of salt. However, part-time employees are now to be found at the professional and managerial levels, with 49 percent of managers reporting that their organization uses such contracts.[22] Official statistics support the managers' accounts. The Labour Force Survey of 1996 indicates part-time working for 25 percent, flexitime for 9 percent, and annual hours for 4 percent of the total workforce. In 1996, 43 percent of the jobs people left were full-time, whereas only 27 percent of the jobs taken by those re-entering the labour market were full-time. If current trends continue, more than half of the working population will very soon be on some form of part-time or flexible contract.

Outsourcing

Outsourcing, likewise, has increased apace, again with the aim of reducing the full-time workforce to those who add value and represent the core competence of the organization. Some 70 percent of managers say that their organization contracts out some of its services.[23] The traditional candidates for outsourcing such as building maintenance, cleaning, transport of goods, security, printing, catering and payroll[24] have now been supplemented by much more professional activities. Evidence from personal experience and media reports indicates that information technology, human resources (e.g. recruitment and training), logistics, and outplacement are all being increasingly contracted out. Thus professional as well as manual staff are finding that their full-time employment with the organization is being replaced by specialist external contractors. They may find themselves employment with these self-same contractors, or they may supply such services themselves as self-employed, and with several clients (Handy's[25] celebrated portfolio career). But they may find themselves unemployed, or on a part-time or temporary contract; for the costs of managing outsourced contracts are making themselves felt. Once again, transaction costs bite back.

Process re-engineering

Finally, a wide range of structures and tools has been employed to enhance productivity, thereby indirectly reducing costs per unit of production. Business process re-engineering is only the latest of such tools, and it has its devotees as has every recent management fad. It also fails to demonstrate the promised benefits in most cases,[26] to which the inevitable response is 'But you didn't do it properly'. The reliable UK data[27] show gradually increasing productivity per person over the last decade, with little loss of productivity even during the depths of the recession in 1990 and 1991. In the recessions of the mid-1970s and the early

1980s, there were in contrast considerable drops. Between 1969 and 1991 it is estimated[28] that UK manufacturing output increased by 10 percent while the workforce was halved.

The maintenance of productivity in the UK during the last recession, however, and the increase overall, are to be attributed to the number of hours worked as well as to increased productivity per hour. The hours worked per week in the UK are the highest in the EU, with males working 45.4 hours compared with an EU norm of 41.1, and females working 40.4 compared to 38.9. Managers in particular claim an increased workload, with nearly 60 percent saying that it had greatly increased over the years 1993–1995.[29] More than half of these managers always or often worked at home in the evenings, and nearly 40 percent said that they always or often worked at weekends. Over 60 percent said their work was a source of stress to them. In this context, the admonition to 'work smarter not harder' is received with a certain degree of resentment. Productivity has been increased, but at a cost – to health, to families and to the institutions of civil society.

RHETORIC: A LATE RUNNER

Given that cost cutting has generally won out at the expense of innovation, we need to be clear as to the likely consequences. These are presented graphically in Figure 2.1, which suggests that cost cutting can become a self-perpetuating cycle. It is partly in order to direct attention away from these long-term consequences that top management employs rhetoric.

It is very easy to get hooked on two uses of the word rhetoric. One appeals to our sense of personal virtue, and is used as the opposite of the word reality: reality is our own view of the situation, rhetoric is the other person's. A second appeals to our need for conspiracy theories: rhetoric is the use of language so as to maintain or enhance the user's power. Discarding such over-simplifications, there are several reasons for top management to be rhetorical at the present juncture.

Types of rhetoric

The first is **aspirational** in nature: 'This is what we're aiming for, and we need to send a clear message to that effect down the organization.' It is not a far step from repeating aspirational messages *ad nauseam* to speak-

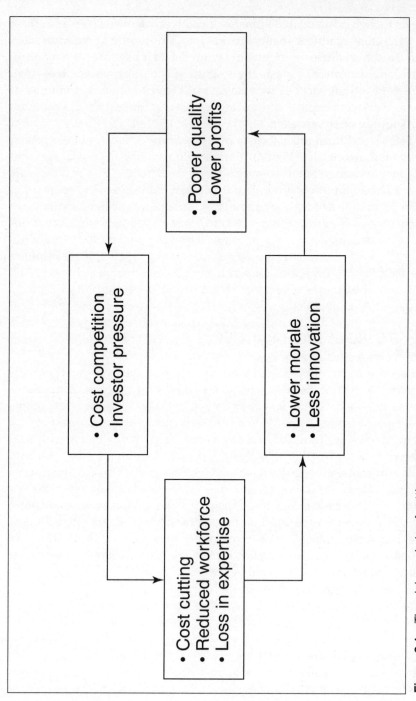

Figure 2.1 The vicious circle of cutting costs

ing as though it is already happening. And it is but a brief step from there to 'marketers' madness'–believing that it is. This is why so much research into human resource management is unreliable: it uses only top management or HR professionals as the sources of the information. They may well believe that because they have 'put the HR architecture in place', because systems exist, then they are being used, and in the way intended. They are often mistaken.

The second form of rhetoric is **presentational**. Instead of being taken in by their own wish list and incurable optimism, top managers aim consciously to change others' perceptions of the situation by what they say or do. The assumption here is that if you succeed in changing employees' perceptions, the actions congruent with those perceptions will follow; for people strive towards a degree of consistency between their perceptions and their actions.

One way of communicating top management's agenda is by changing the artefacts of the organization's culture. So, for example, the introduction of performance-related pay and performance appraisal may be designed to emphasize values of individual achievement and effort, and beliefs that these will be recognized and rewarded. Needless to say, such a form of communication runs the risk of changing behaviour only, rather than values or beliefs; compliance rather than commitment. But top management sometimes mistakes the former for the latter.

Another sort of rhetoric serves the purpose of rationalizing what is going on or what has already happened. So, to use Henry Mintzberg's phrase,[30] rhetoric is a way of making continuing sense of our efforts to adapt to change. To use his term, it is **emerging strategy**. Or with Karl Weick,[31] we can explain strategy as post hoc rationalization: making coherent sense subsequently of actions which were essentially opportunistic at the time. Top management may use such rhetoric to make satisfactory sense to themselves of what they have done. Or they may use it to justify themselves to employees or to the outside world. So, for example, unable to offer job security or career progression any longer, they offer employability in exchange for flexibility as the new employment deal. For employability, read insecurity.

So rhetoric may have a variety of purposes and functions. What is its content? There are currently to be found some very common and general rhetorics, the first of which contrasts the old and the new: old is bad and new is good. Some employees, according to this rhetoric, are bad, because they stupidly believe that the old was good and the new is bad. They are deadwood, and need clearing out, for they cannot change. The old organization, likewise, is bad. It was rigid and hierarchical, and constrained by

New is good, old is bad: the rhetoric of the City, ten years after Big Bang

The Old City	The New City
✳ 9.30am–4.00pm	✳ 7.00am–7.00pm
✳ Liquid lunches	✳ No lunches at all
✳ My word is my bond	✳ Leeson
✳ The old school tie	✳ The brightest and the best
✳ 250,000 employees	✳ 50,000 employees
✳ £100,000 per annum at 60	✳ £100,000 at 28, gone by 40
✳ Equities	✳ Options, derivatives, takeovers
✳ 2% (?) of GDP	✳ 20% of GDP
✳ Brokers 100% British owned	✳ Brokers 45% British owned
✳ Nearly all merchant banks British owned	✳ Rothschild and Schroder

rules. People had a child–adult relationship with their paternalistic employer, and their employment deal was security in exchange for their loyalty. Now they have an adult relationship, and the deal is flexibility for employability. They are self-sufficient and 'career resilient'. In a word, they are good.

A third common rhetoric is that of **human resource management** itself.[32] Resources are by definition those which are to be valued and conserved, but by the same token they are owned and may be utilized. The language is that of economic rationality. That is why the fiction of rational integration of practices among themselves and with business strategy is fundamental. If such integration is a universal objective, then there is likely to be 'one best way',[33] one model of best practice against which we may benchmark ourselves.

The **culture metaphor** is another rhetoric, aiming at hearts and minds. The assumption is that it is desirable to have a single common culture, sharing beliefs and values so that we may all collaborate together to achieve our common goals. The employees can, in the rhetorical double-speak, 'take ownership' of the culture; the cynics have another word for it – brainwashing. This rhetoric assumes that employees' and top management's interests are the same, viz. the financial success of the business. It also assumes that a common culture is possible and beneficial, and can be created by a programme. That programme starts with 'the organization's' vision, mission and values handed down by top management.

A final and related rhetoric is that of the common fate: we are all in this transformation experience together and so we will all sink or swim together. The implication is that we will all share in the pain now and later all enjoy the rewards that our present sufferings will soon make possible. Of course, it is not top management that is inflicting the pain, it is really X, where X can equal any scapegoat from the European Union through to the old deadwood middle managers whom we have just cut out.

It is easy to see how each of these rhetorics can perform the rhetorical functions we have just outlined. The human resource management rhetoric, for example, is a rational and persuasive account of how top management would like employees to be managed: it is mainly aspirational. 'Old is Bad, New is Good' can perform a useful presentational role, in changing the climate to one supporting change; it is also good for rationalizing fads that have failed. And as for the common fate rhetoric, how better to sustain effort in adverse circumstances than by reinvoking the good old Dunkerque spirit: we are all in this together.

RHETORIC'S RESULT: MISTRUST

As we have argued, the motives for these rhetorics (and the many more that we could have detailed) may be varied. What is for sure is that where they fail to correspond to employees' constructions of their own experience, they will give rise to mistrust and cynicism. The credibility gap is crucial.

It is only too easy to spot the credibility gaps, or in some cases yawning chasms, which the rhetorics mentioned earlier can create:

- Old employees cannot all be bad when we have to bring back those who were sacked because their experience is indispensible.

- Old organizational rules and structures must have served some useful purpose when procedures which used to run smoothly now self-destruct.

- If we are all valued human resources, why are we being burned out rather than developed?

- If we are all supposed to share the same values, why is it only top management's values that are on offer?

- If it is equal misery and equal ultimate cake for all, why top management awarded obscene golden handshakes and monster share options,
while we get outplacement (if lucky) and inflation-linked rises only?

So instead of enhancing employees' trust in it by addressing the issues,
top management has forfeited much of it by putting cost cutting ahead of
innovation and quality; and by pretending that it has not. It is worth
exploring further the **nature of trust** at this point, so that the ways in
which it may be restored to support the employment relationship of the
future may become clearer.

The nature of trust

The most fundamental manifestation of trust refers to confidence that
another will fulfil their obligations to you.[34] These may have been explic-
itly undertaken and promised, or they may have been implicit and
assumed. If a friend borrows money, you do not require an explicit
promise to pay it back; it is a societal norm. More subtly, we trust people
to be fair in their reciprocal relationship with us; we expect them, as far
as they are able, to repay us in full. Not only do we trust them to fulfil
their obligations, but we assume that they will do so as far as they are
able in proportion to our own offer to them.

A second manifestation of trust is the confidence that the other will
not try to deceive you:

- by pretending to know something when they do not know it

- by missing out crucial elements of their account

- by putting a highly selective spin onto their account

- by actively deceiving or lying.

Third, we trust people to be able to do things which their position, qualifications, experience and achievements suggest they can do; we do not
stand over them checking up on them all the time, or do it ourselves
because we think they are incapable.

Finally, we trust people not to harm us, and maybe even to care for
our welfare.

As a consequence of favourable trusting experiences, we come to trust people for what they are; we infer personal qualities which make it reasonable for us to trust them. We may infer this trustworthiness by observing the degree to which others trust them, or the characteristics which others attribute to them – trust by proxy.

But our most powerful evidence of all is our own experience of them; have they fulfilled their promises to us so far? Have they lied through their teeth? Have they performed a demanding task well? Have they completed on time?

So trust itself is often **reciprocal**: if others trust me, I may be more likely to trust them; self-disclosure by therapists and counsellors often leads to more disclosure by the client. And the same is true of altruism, or good citizenship.[35] If I think someone has helped me without any expectation of a subsequent favour, I may be more inclined to behave in the same way myself.

Given this more complex account of trust, it is easy to see how degrees of trust may vary within organizations. Top management may have forfeited trust in all these ways as far as the rest of the employees are concerned:

- They may be perceived to have reneged on their obligations under the old psychological contract, and to be offering in the present contract a grossly unfair deal.

- They may have used rhetoric which is so far removed from employees' experience as to constitute an attempt to deceive.

- Assuming that employees have seen through the rhetoric, top management may be perceived to have mismanaged the organization.

- And given their propensity for greed, employees may cease to respect them as people. A recent report found that UK employees respected management less than did employees of any other European country.[36]

And yet it can be seen that some employees may retain high trust in colleagues or immediate line managers who consistently fulfil their obligations to the work group, or who repeatedly demonstrate their capacity to tackle difficult problems and succeed. The danger is, however, that if many people feel insecure and willing to go to any lengths to retain their jobs, they may assume that others feel the same way. Fears that colleagues or subordinates are after one's job are then likely, and trust even in one's co-workers is diminished.

If the amount of trust derived from civil society which employees bring to the workplace is decreasing, and if the top managements of many organizations have forfeited much of the historic social capital that had accrued to them in the past, then the loss of trust is so great as to threaten the norms of collaboration and commitment. The requirement of quality to go beyond your strict obligation and develop a relationship with your internal or external customer is hardly likely to be fulfilled now. Rather, both parties to the employment contract will be wasting time, effort and money trying to ensure that the other fulfils its side of the bargain. Transaction costs are an inevitable consequence of a transactional relationship. So, ironically, the loss of trust resulting from the rhetoric gap has removed the possibility of quality relationships which that very rhetoric was itself trying to encourage.

We may conclude, then, that the loss of trust consequent upon the decrease in social capital in society at large has been exacerbated by the loss of trust within the organizational setting.

Some questions to think about

1. Which of the following management tools have been used by your organization:

   - total quality management
   - performance-related pay
   - vision and mission statements
   - culture change programmes
   - business process re-engineering?

Which of these has been retained in the form in which it was introduced? Which have had their useful parts incorporated into your organization's practices? Which have died a death? What explanation have you got for these outcomes? What have been the intended benefits, the unintended benefits, and the unintended downsides of the tools you have used? What was your role in their introduction? What have been the consequences for you of playing that role?

2. Ask yourself the same questions about the various forms of restructuring that have recently been popular:

   - downsizing
   - delayering
   - flexible contracts

- outsourcing
- matrix or project-based structures.

3. How far down the rhetoric road has your organization gone: is its use of rhetoric primarily aspirational, marketers' madness, presentational or rationalizing? Can you think of any recent examples? Are any of the following rhetorics in frequent use in your organization:

- old is bad, new is good
- human resource management in the service of the business
- a single common culture
- a common fate?

What have been the results of these uses of rhetoric that you are aware of? How have these consequences manifested themselves in employees' attitudes or behaviour?

REFERENCES

1 Institute of Management (1996) *Managing the Management Tools*. London.
2 Storey, J. (1992) 'HRM in action: the truth is out at last'. *Personnel Management* 24 (4): 28–31.
3 Hendry, C. and Pettigrew, A. (1992) 'Patterns of strategic change in the development of human resource management'. *British Journal of Management* 3 (3): 137–56.
4 Sisson, K. and Storey, J. (1993) *Managing Human Resources and Industrial Relations*. Milton Keynes: Open University Press.
5 Hendry, C. and Pettigrew, A. (1992) 'Patterns of strategic change in the development of human resource management'. *British Journal of Management* 3 (3): 137–56.
6 Miller, P. (1987) 'Strategic industrial relations and human resource management: distinction, definition, and recognition'. *Journal of Management Studies* 24 (4): 347–61.
7 Legge, K. (1995) *Human Resource Management: Rhetorics and Realities*. London: Macmillan.
8 Thompson, M. (1992) 'Pay and performance: the employer experience'. Brighton: Institute for Manpower Studies, Report 218.
9 New Earnings Survey (1996). London: HMSO.
10 Thompson, M. (1993) 'Pay and performance: the employee experience'. Brighton: Institute for Manpower Studies, Report 258.
11 Wilkinson, A., Marchington, M., Goodman, J. and Ackers, P. (1992) 'Total quality management and employee involvement'. *Human Resource Management Journal* 2 (4): 1–20.

12 Oliver, N. and Wilkinson, B. (1992) *The Japanization of British Industry: New Developments in the 1990s*, 2nd edn. Oxford: Blackwell.
13 Labour Force Survey (1995). London: HMSO.
14 Hirsh, W. and Jackson, C. (1996) 'Strategies for career development: promise, practice, and pretence'. Brighton: Institute for Employment Studies, Report 305.
15 Tamkin, P., Barber, L. and Hirsh, W. (1995) 'Personal development plans: case studies of practice'. Brighton: Institute for Employment Studies, Report 280.
16 Connor, H. and Pollard, E. (1996) 'What do graduates really do?' Brighton: Institute for Employment Studies, Report 308.
17 Purcell, K. and Pitcher, J. (1996) *Great Expectations: The New Diversity of Graduate Skills and Aspirations*. Manchester: Careers Services Unit.
18 Wheatley, M. (1992) *The Future of Middle Management*. Corby: BIM Press.
19 Labour Force Survey (1995). London: HMSO.
20 Gregg, P. and Wadsworth, J. (1996) 'A short history of labour turnover, job tenure, and job security, 1975–1993'. *Oxford Review of Economic Policy* 11 (1): 73–90.
21 Institute of Management (1995) *Survey of Long Term Employment Strategies*. London.
22 Institute of Management (1996) *Flexibility and Fairness: A Survey of Managers' Attitudes to Part-time Employment and Part-time Employees*. London.
23 Institute of Management (1995) *Survey of Long Term Employment Strategies*. London.
24 Millward, N. (1994) *The New Industrial Relations?* London: Policy Studies Institute.
25 Handy, C. (1985) *The Future of Work*. Oxford: Blackwell.
26 Mumford, E. and Hendricks, R. (1996) 'Business process re-engineering RIP'. *People Management* 2 (9): 22–9.
27 Beatson, M. (1995) *Labour Market Flexibility*. London: Employment Department.
28 Hamel, G. and Prahalad, C.K. (1994) 'Competing for the future'. *Harvard Business Review* 72 (4): 122–8.
29 Institute of Management (1995) *Survival of the Fittest*. London.
30 Mintzberg, H. (1994) *The Rise and Fall of Strategic Planning: Reconceiving Roles for Planning, Plans, and Planners*. New York: Free Press.
31 Weick, K.E. (1995) *Sensemaking in Organizations*. Thousand Oaks, CA: Sage.
32 Legge, K. (1995) *Human Resource Management: Rhetorics and Realities*. London: Macmillan.
33 Taylor, F.W. (1911) *The Principles of Scientific Management*. New York: W.W. Norton.
34 Gouldner, A.W. (1960) 'The norm of reciprocity: a preliminary statement'. *American Sociological Review* 25: 161–79.
35 Bryan, J.H. and Test, A.T. (1967) 'Models and helping: naturalistic studies in aiding behaviour'. *Journal of Personality and Social Psychology* 6: 400–407.
36 International Survey Research (1996) *Employee Satisfaction: Tracking European Trends*. London.

Personal survival stakes 3

SECURITY AND TRUST

The positive side

Trust is a social virtue. It permeates all relationships, especially those fundamental social and emotional bonds which are forged in our infancy. That is why it is so important for organizations, since, like families, organizations are social entities or they are nothing. Trust of colleagues, of line management, and of top management is a necessary condition for collaboration and leadership. Yet the social virtue of trust is greatly conditional upon a much more personal and individual feeling: security.

Trust and security have a symbiotic relationship to each other.[1] If I am feeling secure, I am more likely to take the risk involved in trusting someone else. The loss I might incur if my trust is misplaced means less to me if I feel in a position of personal security. I am more likely to act on the assumption that my action will be reciprocated, and that my initial commitment will not be taken advantage of. I am more confident in colleagues' ability to perform, rather than do something myself in case it goes wrong and I carry the can. Maybe I am even more likely to perceive another as trustworthy rather than to question his or her motives.

And of course it works the other way round as well. When I have others whom I can trust, I feel more secure. I know they will not betray my confidences, seek to deceive me, or renege on an agreement. I feel that they are capable of helping me, and that they will certainly do so when the need arises. I will even be prepared to do something for them without any prospect of any immediate reciprocation, since I am so confident that they will be there when I need them.[2]

The negative side

But the negative side of the coin is equally true. Where trust is scarce and perceived contracts have been reneged upon, I will feel insecure.[3]

Where I believe that my social contract with the state and my psychological contract with my employer have both been broken by the other, I will
lose confidence in contracting in general. And conversely, and much more
importantly for the employment relationship, the less secure and confident I feel, the less likely I am to trust another.

We have already argued in Chapter 1 that trust as a major element of
social capital has decreased in our society; and we have demonstrated in
Chapter 2 that organizations have further dissipated that social capital
by their actions, their rhetoric and the gap between the two over the last
decade. In this chapter we will outline yet another source of lack of trust:
the increasing personal insecurity that assaults individuals in modern
western societies. Important to note here is that feelings of insecurity are
not an invention of the media, nor a 'finger in the wind' guestimate by
commentators. All opinion poll evidence indicates that there are very
high levels of job insecurity. In mid-1996, for example, 40 percent of
employees feared for their jobs, and 60 percent alleged that insecurity
was rising.[4] Furthermore, these feelings of insecurity are now typical of
middle as well as working class respondents. In a Gallup poll,[5] 52 percent of middle class respondents and 68 percent of working class respondents said they felt economically insecure, while the figures for the
perceived possibility of unemployment were 31 percent and 40 percent
respectively. The class gap was far greater, reports Gallup, than during
the early 1980s. As for the future, 51 percent of the middle class and 60
percent of the working class respondents believed that another recession
is possible before the turn of the century. Very recent evidence from the
Institute of Personnel and Development suggests some decrease in insecurity during the present boomlet.

Economists and politicians are baffled by the current feelings of job
insecurity, asking how people can feel insecure when unemployment levels have been decreasing in the UK for four or five years. If their objective security has been reliably increasing recently, and if it has only
decreased slightly over the last 20 years as a whole, why are they so irra-
tional? The answers we propose are:

- First, because they are justifiably frightened of what will happen to
  them if they are made redundant.

- Second, because they feel insecure about a whole range of life supports
  in addition to employment.

- Finally, because job insecurity relates to identity as well as to income.

It is as if Joshua Slocum had come so close to being sunk as he rounded the Cape that he lost all confidence in his seamanship and his ability to survive another onslaught of nature. He starts to wonder whether he is a seaman at all, or at least, whether he is man enough to carry on. And then he learns that his next port of call has shut its harbour to him, as it is using it for something much more important: a fleet of Japanese merchant ships. Even the stoutest of mariners can feel despondent in these circumstances.

SOME SAILORS FEEL SAFE: OTHERS ARE TERRIFIED

The facts about unemployment and redundancy in the UK are reasonably clear, despite more than twenty changes in the method of calculating unemployment introduced by the Conservative governments of 1979–1997. From a very low base in the early 1970s, unemployment rose to about 3 million in 1986 and to a subsequent peak of nearly 3 million again in 1993, since when it has steadily but slowly declined.[6] The peaks are due to increased redundancies during recessions. Even when there were booms, as in the late 1980s, there was no sudden huge increase in employment. So while the ocean's swell has grown, we have gradually got used to the choppy seas as a fact of sailing life in the late twentieth century. The threatening waves are there all the time: it is always Cape Horn.

Yet some have much more reason to fear shipwreck than others. In spring 1995, the overall unemployment rate was 8.6 percent, with women at 6.8 percent, men in general at 10.1 percent, men aged 16–19 at 15.3 percent, and those without formal qualifications at 14 percent.[7] These figures, of course, conceal the changing nature of employment: between March and September 1993, 113,000 full-time jobs vanished, and 210,000 part-time jobs were created.[8] By the end of 1995, nearly 25 percent of those in work were working part time. Joshua Slocum would have been horrified: all these weekend sailors pushing aside the professionals, and most of them women to boot.

Global versus UK trends

However, these figures are relatively moderate compared with some other countries. In 1990/91, Canada, the USA, Australia, Norway and Denmark all had higher proportions of the working population becoming unemployed than did the UK.[9] Furthermore, when we look at those employed in the UK as a percentage of the total population aged 15–64, there was an increase of 2.2 percent between 1972 and 1992, only slightly

less than the OECD average increase of 3.8 percent.[10] For some occupations, such as managerial, professional and associated professional occupations, a shortfall is actually predicted by the year 2000; it is in the
clerical, secretarial, and skilled and unskilled manual occupations that
surplus labour will occur.[11] It is all done by instruments now, Slocum
would complain; where has the real seamanship gone?

This mixed picture is particularly noticeable when we look at the data
about the length of tenure in organizations.[12] The median length of
employment within an organization was 5.8 years in 1975 and 4.9 years
in 1993. In 1993, then, around 50 percent of the working population had
spent more than five years in the same organization, and around 30 percent more than ten years. However, these figures conceal a marked fall in
average male length of tenure of 20 percent since 1975, but a rise in female
tenure of 10 percent.

So there are marked socio-economic class and gender differences in
the experience of redundancy and unemployment, but overall the position has not changed markedly for the worse for the majority in recent
years. What has changed is what becomes of you if you are made redundant – what happens when you fall over the side of the ship. Entry positions for the currently unemployed have become increasingly unstable
and low paid. The jobs available are increasingly likely to be part time
and temporary, with full-time jobs becoming ever more scarce. While 63
percent of all work in 1992/3 consisted of full-time permanent jobs, only
30 percent of new jobs were of this nature.[13] Indeed, between 1992 and
1996, one-half of the jobs newly created were part time, while of the full-
time jobs that were created, nearly one-half were temporary rather than
'permanent'.

Moreover, only 60 percent of those leaving registered unemployment
went back into work. The rest entirely lost touch with the labour market,
reducing unemployment without increasing employment.[14] They sank
into the murky depths without trace. For the majority of those in part-
time work, there are fewer than 17 hours per week on offer – survival on
the liferaft with hardly any rations left. Furthermore, relatively few part-
time and temporary workers have the statutory minimum employment
rights, for which the qualification period is now two years. And you are
likely to take a 33 percent salary loss from your previous job if you move
from redundancy through a period of unemployment to a new job; so
even if a rescue vessel does pick you up, conditions on board are pretty
grim. Once you get to be really poor, i.e. below half the average income,
you have a terrible problem in getting better off again; nearly half those
below the line are above it a year later, but one-third slip down again in
the following year.[15] Those in peril on the sea.

Is part-time employment merely a short-term stepping-stone on the path back to full-time work? It seems not. Only 14 percent of those leaving full-time work are in a similar full-time post three months later; 58 percent are not in work at all.[16] There simply are insufficient full-time jobs to meet the demand. What is more, those who are getting back into work are likely to be those with a working partner; the number of households without any working member at all has tripled since 1975, and is now over 20 percent of all households.[17] Of course, we should not assume that all those in part-time jobs are trying to get full-time ones; it is likely that for the majority of part-timers it is the preferred option. But for those who do want to make the move back to full-time work, the prospects are bleak. And government training schemes have hitherto offered little hope of getting back to full-time work; two-thirds of trainees are on benefit within nine months of completion of training.

Redundancy and dismissal

Over and above the threat of redundancy, people at work feel insecure regarding their risk of maltreatment by their employer. Unions which have traditionally protected employees against unjust treatment by management have decreased in membership and power over the last fifteen years. Legislation has limited various employee rights regarding unfair dismissal,[18] yet the number of unfair dismissal cases has increased from just below 20,000 in 1990 to 40,000 in 1995.

So those currently in full-time work may not have a very high objective probability of redundancy. But when they look over the side of the ship and see what happens if it strikes the rocks of redundancy, then there is little doubt why they feel insecure. And as the number of full-time jobs falls, the number at risk rises. The penalties attached to job loss have risen, and Charles Handy's[19] picture of the portfolio career can be seen as a sick joke to all but a section of the professional classes. Few can afford a luxury cruise where you disembark where and when the fancy takes.

SAFETY AT SEA

Psychologically speaking, job insecurity is unlikely to have an isolated effect. Rather, given the centrality of work to people's economic, social, and personal well-being, it must be seen as a part only of a more pervasive sense of insecurity. Few sailors feel really safe these days.

The social contract

Consider the social contract, that unspoken but powerful deal that we believe we used to have with the state, and with its tangible representatives, among them the government of the day. The post-war settlement was based upon a deal whereby we thought we secured the necessities of life (education, healthcare, housing, pension and unemployment benefit) in exchange for the contributions we made in tax and national insurance. Recently the rules of the game have changed: the state offers far less, yet we older ones have contributed our part of the bargain already. Now we rush to insure our lives and our health, our mortgages and our salaries.

Even middle-class managers and professionals feel insecure financially. Over 50 percent of managers were concerned about financial pressures, while negative equity affected 15 percent in a recent Institute of Management Survey.[20] Since 1989, bricks and mortar, the traditional investment of the middle class, has dipped and then stagnated in value, only to start rising again in 1997. By the same token, our level of personal debt, much of it incurred in buying those self-same bricks and mortar, has quadrupled since 1980.

State pensions

As for state pensions, they have decreased from a high of 27 percent of average earnings in 1982 to 16 percent, falling still further in 1996. Meanwhile everyone is living longer: by the year 2001 the number of nonagenarians will have doubled since 1990, and by 2031 it will have trebled. In the meantime, the number of local authority places in homes for the elderly has been decreasing since 1986. How are we going to support our parents, and then ourselves, we wonder, in pensions, in housing and in healthcare? Without an income, we have no hope of doing so. We have just got to carry on working . . . or win the lottery.

Declining social institutions

Among the many instances of declining social and political institutions which have hitherto offered a degree of security, **the family** is perhaps the most important to people. The visible and traditional indices of family life all indicate a breakdown of structures and relationships, although many would argue that other features of family life which are not traditionally measured are providing alternative sources of security and love. Be that as it may, 22 percent of families in the UK were cared for by a lone parent in 1993, as opposed to less than 8 percent in 1971.[21] The vast majority of these single parents are mothers, who are getting steadily poorer. Again, it is not just their own marriage that people are worried about; it is their children's, their parents' and their friends' marriages too.

Protection against violence in civil society and against injustice in the workplace has likewise decreased. Perceiving the increasing fragmentation of our society, people's fear of crime has exceeded its incidence. Nevertheless, crime rates have indeed increased over the last four decades, with 1 percent suffering a recorded crime against person or property in 1951, compared with 10 percent in 1995. In 1979 there were 2.3 million recorded offences, today there are 5.4 million, and the perpetrators are much less likely to be arrested, prosecuted, or convicted. Crime rates are, unsurprisingly, higher among the unemployed, and are four times higher in the most deprived council estates than in suburbia. Highly publicized violent crime by adolescent and juvenile offenders adds to felt insecurity. As with redundancy, fear about crime seems to exceed its actual occurrence.

In sum, the whole maritime environment has changed to being a more hostile, less safe one. We are each sailing on a sea where the lighthouses have been shut down, where we constantly fear pirates appearing over the horizon, where sea captains are often cruel and tyrannical and where the seaman's rest and retirement homes have been privatized. No wonder sailing is not much fun these days.

MARINER OR MOUSE?

Insecurity is about fundamentals. It is about physical fundamentals such as food, health and housing. And it is also about psychological fundamentals. The present insecurity is not only anxiety about losing the necessities of life. It is also an existential anxiety about fundamental elements of our identity.[22] Work identities may consist of different elements for different people. Some identify with their employer: 'I'm a Rolls Royce man through and through.' Some define themselves by their occupation or their performance: 'I'm a chartered accountant', or 'I won the salesperson of the year award.' For others, yet again, their work gives them a purpose: 'I'm the main breadwinner for this family', or 'The rewards aren't high but at least I'm doing a bit of good for people.' Work also gives a frame for time and activity,[23] and it provides new relationships and experiences.

Of course, job insecurity is the main threat to these elements of our identity. But there are other trends too which are changing the landscape:

- **Manufacturing jobs are giving way to service sector jobs**. In 1954 manufacturing employed 34.5 percent of the workforce; by the year 2000 this figure is expected to be only 16 percent.[24] During the latest recession, manufacturing lost 820,000 jobs, while the service sector lost only 340,000. By the year 2000 there will probably be a further loss of manufacturing jobs of 825,000, but a gain of 1,325,000 service jobs. It is the skilled and unskilled operatives in the manufacturing sector who are most at risk.

- **There is an associated shift from manual to knowledge work**. Managerial, professional, associate professional and technical jobs are expected to constitute 41 percent of all jobs in AD2000, an increase of 1,700,000 (6 percent) over the present. Between 1971 and AD2000 manual jobs will have decreased from 47 percent of all jobs to 27 percent.

- **There is an overwhelming difference between men and women**.[25] In 1984 there were 9.6 million women in employment, and by 1993 this figure had grown to 11 million. Over the same period, the number of men actually fell, from 13.5 to 13.3 million. Hence men are far more likely to become unemployed, with the increase in unemployment in 1992 being composed of more than 80 percent men. Of course, part of this gender shift is bound up with the increase in part-time working, since in 1996 45 percent of female employees were part-timers, but only 8 percent of males.

- **Older people are much less likely to be in work now than they used to be**.[26] In 1970 some 90 percent of those aged over 55 were in work, and even 20 percent of the over 65s. By 1989 the figure for the over 55s was less than 70 percent. By spring 1996 the activity rate for men aged 50–64 and women aged 50–59 was only 68.4 percent. Yet the demographic facts are that the workforce of AD2006 will be older overall than that of today, with a particular boom in those aged 35–44.

- **There is a major shift from employment in large organizations to smaller ones**.[27] By 1989 42.3 percent of employees worked in organizations of fewer than 50 people, and this percentage is growing annually. In the late 1980s firms of ten or fewer accounted for nearly half of all new jobs created. If small is beautiful, then the world of work is becoming a joy for ever.

- **There is a noteworthy shift from the public to the private sector**. The 29 percent of the workforce who were public servants in 1982 decreased to 23 percent in 1992. The official values in the public sector are now those of quasi markets and cost reduction rather than those of service. The rhetoric of 'choice for the customer' conceals a crucial debate about who the ultimate 'customer' is, and whose interests are paramount.

Many would argue that some or indeed all of these trends are to the good. It is good to retire younger (so long, that is, as you have a pension). It is good that so many of those hard grinding manual jobs have gone. It is good that more and more women have jobs (provided that they want them). It is good that the public sector should attend more to its efficiency and value for money. Whether or not these trends are beneficial to individuals, to organizations and to civil society is open to debate. What is abundantly clear, however, is that the identity and self-esteem of some sections of society are being threatened by them.

Identity and status under threat

Many men, and particularly those in manual manufacturing jobs, have long thought of themselves as the main family breadwinner. Given that their work carried low social status, their identity was not bound up so much in its nature as in its purpose: to provide the necessities of life and some of its pleasures for oneself and one's dependants. The trends from a male to a female workforce, from manufacturing to service, and from manual to professional have shaken this identity to the core. What it means to be a man has altered in half a generation for these casualties of the employment earthquake. In the USA we can see the consequences in high crime rates, with 2 percent of the male workforce in prison and 10 percent passing through the criminal justice system. Aggression is one of the more obvious ways for men to react when their identities are threatened.

Other identities too are under threat. When you have accumulated a lifetime's work experience, it is devastating to have to stop work at 50 and see your 25-year-old successors making the same old mistakes. When you are a civil servant or a health worker or a teacher, whose vocation has been to serve others, it is shattering to have one's lifetime values challenged and one's work denigrated as a mere cost to be reduced. When you have spent your working life going the extra mile for a large blue-chip company that gave you security, a career, and status in the community, it is deeply wounding to be cast out into a world where no-one has even heard of your new employer (if you can find one).

Joshua Slocum would be horrified. Is he a mariner, proud of his call-ing, or has he become a mere seamouse, searching for crumbs in others' vessels? In his indomitable way he would have survived; but few of us are Slocums.

RESTORING TRUST

The picture we have been painting so far is one of almost unremitting gloom. It is a far cry from the inspirational hype of management texts, most of which suffer from marketers' madness: the fantasy that if you want something enough, it comes to pass. Yet those employers who value their employees sufficiently highly to spend money on finding out how they feel, tell a common tale in private.[28] Even in many of these generally worthy companies, never has employee morale been lower, and never has the gap between top management's attitudes and those of the work-force been greater. It is better to face up to these facts than to hope to talk up morale by being unfailingly cheerful and optimistic. It is alright for them up there, say the troops.

That is why the picture we have painted may seem alien to the exper-ience of most of our readers, for most will belong to the managerial and professional core of organizations. While they will acknowledge the long hours and stress, they will nevertheless enjoy the challenge and the responsibility. Many thrive on uncertainty and the challenges and oppor-tunities that it brings. And Thatcher's children may hold very different expectations of their employers and the world of work from those of their parents. Transaction rather than relationship may be the name of their game.

Trust, collaboration and rhetoric

Nevertheless, we return to our fundamental argument. Trust is necessary for collaboration at work. Collaboration is increasingly necessary for organizational survival. Trust is a decreasing element of social capital in western societies. Western organizations have dissipated what little trust they did inherit. The sense of personal security necessary for trust has also been largely destroyed.

The conclusion is inescapable. The very first task of top manage-ment is to seek to re-establish trust. As Lynda Gratton maintains on the basis of her Leading Edge research project:

> Competative advantage will be gained only when
> employees trust their company, when their aspirations
> match the company's strategy, and when their hopes
> stand a chance of being met.[29]

Our earlier analysis of trust makes it evident how they may set about this monumental task. First, they will do what they say they are going to do; and they will be doing what they say they are doing. Putting it the other way round, they will say what they are intending to do and tell the truth about what they are actually doing. Hence top managements will be miserly with their promises, but they will follow them through and fulfil them whatever the cost. They will never say they are doing something when in fact they are merely hanging a fig leaf over their nakedness. They will inform employees about what they are intending to do and why. And they will not conceal or misrepresent what they are actually doing. Above all, they will stop expecting employees to go the extra mile over and above their obligations when they themselves have failed to fulfil their own obligations as promised.

All forms of rhetoric are actively hostile to both these activities; they must be avoided like the plague. Hence top managements will be very wary of 'the next big idea'. They will give up on messianic visions and symbolic gestures. They will resist management fads, however powerfully they are marketed.[30] They will banish buzzwords from their vocabulary. So much of the recent rhetoric has come to mean the precise opposite of what it was intended to mean that any abstract idea such as empowerment or self-development now serves merely to increase cynicism. In business, as in politics, rhetoric is out. Rhetoric enhances mistrust, since the motive of deceit is usually attributed to the rhetorician, even when persuasion or encouragement may have been intended.

Next, top management will enhance trust by their own business actions. If they can give good reasons for their decisions and policies, if they are seen to solicit and take good advice and if they are as consistent and predictable over time as fits with change, then they will be trusted and respected as good managers. If they likewise demonstrate trust in their employees by respecting their skills and treating them as capable of solving problems for themselves and managing their own work, then such trust will be reciprocated.

Finally, employees will trust top management more if they respect them as people. One good way for top managers to forfeit such trust is by making it transparent that they are essentially greedy and inequitable. Another is by engaging in small and mean-minded interventions which obviously fail to address the breadth of the organization's issues. And a final one is by failing to ask or listen to what all employees have to say, and by refusing to hear or give bad news.

We have lapsed from analysis into prescription. The next two chapters, however, demonstrate why trust is becoming so vital. For they show that the business transitions faced by organizations and the career transitions faced by individuals are ever more frequent and profound. Both parties depend on each other if they are to make these transitions successfully; **mutual trust is of the essence**.

Some questions to think about

1. Do you regularly assess the level of morale and motivation among your employees? Do you pay attention to the trends over time in these assessments? Do you use them to test various hypotheses about why morale might be increasing or decreasing? Or to test the impact of any interventions the organization has made?

2. Do you assess the levels of job and psychological security felt by employees? Do you know the extent to which security contributes to general morale?

3. What effects do you believe insecurity has upon performance? What effects do you think the board believes insecurity has upon performance? How might you demonstrate these effects persuasively?

4. What actions if any can an organization undertake to reduce insecurity?

REFERENCES

1 Brockner, J. (1988) 'The effects of work lay-offs on survivors: research, theory and practice', in B.M. Staw and L.L Cummings (eds) *Research in Organizational Behavior* vol. 10. Greenwich, CT: JAI Press.
2 Organ, D.W. (1990) 'The motivational basis of organizational citizenship behavior', in B.M. Staw and L.L Cummings (eds) *Research in Organizational Behavior* vol. 12. Greenwich, CT: JAI Press.
3 Morrison, E.W. and Robinson, S.L. (1997) 'When employees feel betrayed: a model of how psychological contract violation develops'. *Academy of Management Review* 22 (1): 226–56.

4 Gregg, P. (1996) 'We work, it hurts: why job fears are rising'. *The Observer*, 16 June.
5 *Daily Telegraph*, 9 January 1994.
6 Beatson, M. (1995) *Labour Market Flexibility*. London: Department of Employment.
7 Labour Force Survey (1995). London: HMSO.
8 Labour Force Survey (1995). London: HMSO.
9 Beatson, M. (1995) *Labour Market Flexibility*. London: Department of Employment.
10 Beatson, M. (1995) *Labour Market Flexibility*. London: Department of Employment.
11 IER (1994) *Review of the Economy and Employment: Occupational Assessment*. Warwick: University of Warwick.
12 Gregg, P. and Wadsworth, J. (1996) 'A short history of labour turnover, job tenure, and job security, 1975–1993'. *Oxford Review of Economic Policy* 11 (1): 73–90.
13 Beatson, M. (1995) *Labour Market Flexibility*. London: Department of Employment.
14 Beatson, M. (1995) *Labour Market Flexibility*. London: Department of Employment.
15 Jenkins, S. et al. (1996) *Changing Places: Income Mobility and Poverty Dynamics in Britain*. Colchester: University of Essex.
16 Gregg, P. and Wadsworth, J. (1996) 'A short history of labour turnover, job tenure, and job security, 1975–1993'. *Oxford Review of Economic Policy* 11 (1): 73–90.
17 Gregg, P. and Wadsworth, J. (1996) 'A short history of labour turnover, job tenure, and job security, 1975–1993'. *Oxford Review of Economic Policy* 11 (1): 73–90.
18. Legge, K. (1995) *Human Resource Management: Rhetorics and Realities*. London: Macmillan.
19 Handy, C. (1985) *The Future of Work*. Oxford: Blackwell.
20 Institute of Management (1996) *Are Managers under Stress?* London.
21 General Household Survey (1994). London: HMSO.
22 Hartley, J., Jacobson, D., Klandermans, B. and Van Vuuren, T. (1991) *Job Insecurity: Coping with Jobs at Risk*. London: Sage.
23 Jahoda, M. (1982) *Employment and Unemployment: A Social Psychological Analysis*. Cambridge: Cambridge University Press.
24 IER (1994) *Review of the Economy and Employment: Occupational Assessment*. Warwick: University of Warwick.
25 Ellison, R. (1995) 'Labour force projections for countries and regions in the United Kingdom, 1995–2006'. *Employment Gazette* 103: 303–314.
26 *Employment Gazette*, April 1994.
27 *Employment Gazette*, February 1992.
28 Storey, J. (1995) 'Employment policies and practices in UK clearing banks: an overview.' *Human Resource Management Journal* 5 (4): 24–43.

29 Gratton, L. (1997) 'Tomorrow people.' *People Management* 3 (15): 22–7.
30 Huczynski, A.A. (1993) 'Explaining the succession of management fads'. *International Journal of Human Resource Management* 4 (2): 443–64.

Organizational strategy: rational or rationalization? 4

STRATEGY IS ABOUT TRANSITIONS

'Gloom, doom, and nostalgia, and even the nostalgia's not what it used to be' will be the charge against our first three chapters. What we have actually argued is that while the old career deals could not survive, there was often lost with them the condition necessary for any future success-ful employment relationship: a degree of mutual trust. However, we have not yet concluded our realistic analysis of the context of careers. In the next two chapters we will address the organizational context in more detail. In particular, we will focus on the increasing frequency of transi-tions, both at the organizational and at the individual level. We argue that the fundamental reality of organizational life is already one of con-stant business transitions, and that these will become yet more frequent. The inevitable consequence is that individual career transitions will also happen more often. Our analysis will conclude with a statement of the enormity of the task of career management in the light of the decrease in trust and the increase in transitions. For successful transition requires more, not less trust.

Strategy as a process

Studies of strategic business behaviour in organizations[1] suggest that we will be wasting our time if we think in terms of long-term business plan-ning. Strategy is, to use a nice euphemism, 'emergent', by which is meant that it is adaptive behaviour which hopefully anticipates, but often lags, changes in the business, political, and social environments. Strategy is not a product, but a process. A long-range strategic plan usually becomes obsolete before it can be used, and anyway it is next to impossible to know what to plan for except uncertainty. What we see instead ever more frequently are opportunistic mergers or acquisitions. These usually imply major change for the senior party and total upheaval for the junior one. The transformation is to an entirely new entity, yet there has seldom been time enough for the implications for organizational structures and HR processes to be worked out in advance.

Equal difficulty arises if we seek to discover general types of business strategy for which we can then design the appropriate HR strategy.[2] Little support has been found for the simple categories that have been proposed, for example, defender, analyser, prospector and reactor.[3] This is primarily because organizations' responses to their environment have been far less consistent and clearcut than these idealised categories imply. What is more, HR policies and practices that cohere with each other and with the business strategy are more likely to be prescriptive ideals than on the ground realities.[4] We agree with Weick's[5] judgement that formal strategic statements are more likely to be post hoc rationalizations than planned directions.

Finally, and here we are becoming more controversial, we believe that HR strategic thinking should not be based primarily on ideas about what 'the' organization of the future will be like. While large western multinational organizations may have many responses to environmental changes in common,[6][7] why should we believe that others will necessarily follow suit? Why, for example, should we expect organizations of all sizes and in every country to decentralize? Why should we expect them all to shed labour? Will hierarchies universally flatten out? Will leadership generally be distributed throughout the organization? Will contracting out all but the core activities become universal? Will budgetary responsibility be devolved further and further down whatever line there is left? We doubt it. We believe that organizational forms will fragment and adapt each to its own market and cultural territory. Some will become virtual networks; others will retain a hierarchical structure and a local presence. Some will consist mostly of knowledge workers; others will require face-to-face (or voice-to-voice) staff providing a round-the-clock service. The single thing that they will all have in common is that they will have to change as the nature of their territory changes.

The conclusion is inescapable: **the core business activity of any organization is the leadership and management of the processes of change**. Strategy is about process more than it is about content. It is about making continuous transitions from one state to the next. In Joshua Slocum's terms, it is about setting a course and then adapting it frequently to accord with the conditions. On occasion, it will mean changing our mind about the identity of the next port of call. Rarely, it may mean asking, in the light of the captain's scurvy and the long-term unseaworthiness of the good ship *Spray*, whether we should really be in the global circumnavigation business at all. Asking this most fundamental question of all is a last resort, though; circumnavigation was Slocum's raison d'être. In the absence of formal strategic plans, organizations too need to have a central purpose. It is the most radical change of all to question its correctness.

Military readers will object that we are confusing strategy with tactics; making continuous transitions is hardly the stuff of strategy. Today's business people would reply that any attempt to survey the scene, reflect on activity and anticipate external change justifies the label 'strategy'.

THE PROCESS OF TRANSITION

If strategy is about how to lead and manage change rather than being changed willy-nilly, then its key component is the process of transition. If this process is a continuous one, then there is no cut-off point to a change process at which we reach a lasting steady state. We can never 'get back to normal'. Rather, we can at best refer to points at which one cycle of transition ends and the next starts. Except that even this snapshot is not often possible, since normally another transition cycle has started while the previous one is still running its course.

Furthermore, not only are transition cycles overlapping each other sequentially, there are other sequences of cycles running at the same time. These are abstract notions, but we can put more flesh on them if we consider a typical medium or large financial sector organization of today. Such an organization may well be in transition at several different levels of analysis at the same time: at the levels of its products and markets; of its alliances or takeovers; of its structures and systems; and of the design of work roles, as shown in Figure 4.1.

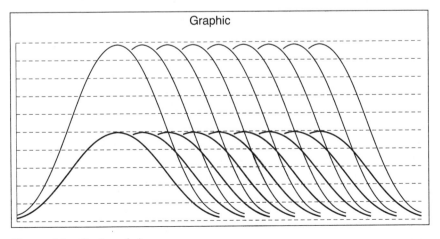

Figure 4.1 Cycles of change

Exbankcorp

Deregulation has enabled the organization to offer any financial service in any marketplace it wishes, and it has decided to diversify. So it is now nearing the end of the process of transition from a single product line to a portfolio of products. And yet it has probably only just started on the process of deciding which of its potential markets it should aim for. Deregulation has also made it vulnerable to takeover by foreign predators, however, so it is also in the transition between standing alone and forging defensive alliances with others equally fearful of takeover. Product and market differentiation has led it to engage in a fundamental structural change, devolving from a strong corporate centre into separate businesses. These will each be in the process of developing appropriate policies and systems to meet their very different needs. This transition in itself requires what remains of the corporate centre to decide which systems need to be retained at a corporate level, and develop them to meet the requirements both of the businesses and of the centre.

The transition from a single product to a multiple portfolio has led to a fundamental redesign of work. Such functions as marketing and selling have gained a new prominence, and information technology is removing power from experts and putting it at the disposal of frontline salespersons in the form of expert systems. Indeed, such organizations now depend on their telesales staff as the most important business getters, and are in the process of learning to treat them as such rather than as employees at the lowest promotional grade. Given the need to meet customers' requirements at any time of the day or night, they are rapidly developing a range of arrangements for flexible working that suit these new aristocrats of the workforce. At the same time, they are seeking to establish what professional and managerial competencies they will need to devise, and implement new products and services.

Thus we have sequences of transitions at several different levels of analysis. In each of these sequences, the next transition overlaps the previous one. So, for example, there are transition cycles around structure and around alliances; the transition from corporate centre to different businesses has not yet bedded down before the corporate centre is seeking out alliances which may profoundly affect the product market or structure of one or more of the businesses. A bank may diversify into an insurance business among others, but while that business is still inventing itself, an alliance with an insurance company may be developed which adds to its potential markets.

Consider a sequence of transitions at the level of the design of work. A development process to enable clerical grades to progress via supervisory to managerial roles may be taking shape, but just when these new style supervisors are beginning to come through into middle management, it is decided to develop self-managing teams of telesales staff, since it is believed that they work better if left to manage themselves. So new transitions can assist or hinder the completion of previous ones.

ORGANIZATIONAL TRANSITIONS

Organizational change, then, can be represented as a set of sequences of overlapping transitions. Some of these are so profound, according to some commentators, as to merit the label 'transformation' rather than transition.[8] The corporate change from retail bank to financial supermarket might deserve such a title. Such transformations require changes in fundamental assumptions about what the business is about and the reordering of value priorities. Yet whatever the level of each transition, we argue that it is likely to involve the organization in four phases of activity. These organizational transition phases are identical with the phases of personal career transitions proposed by Nicholson and West,[9] [10] these being:

- preparation
- encounter
- adjustment
- stabilization.

However, in a sequence of transitions, preparation for the next transition may occur simultaneously with stabilization of the previous one. Or the overlap may be even greater, with the next preparation and encounter occurring while the previous adjustment is still taking place and the stabilization stage is entirely lost.

The effective management of transitional change can sometimes be found. It requires the manager to:

- facilitate the phases of each transition so that, for example, preparation is sufficient to support encounter and adjustment

- mesh in the first phase(s) of the next transition with the later phase(s) of the previous one so that they do not conflict
- coordinate the different levels of transition, e.g. transitions at the structural level with those at the level of role design
- facilitate learning how to make transitions successfully
- limit the number of transitions to those essential to organizational adaptation, so as to avoid 'change fatigue'.

Frequent examples of failures to manage transitions in these five ways indicate their importance:

- Although the City's Big Bang was signalled well in advance, most staff were ill prepared for the shock of competition, especially foreign competition.

- Management initiatives such as total quality management were still bedding down when preparation for a potentially incompatible subsequent initiative such as individual performance-related pay was commenced.

- HR professionals were still operating as administrators of central corporate processes when devolved businesses were wanting them to act as consultants to line managers.

- Reviews of process and outcomes were not held after the first wave of downsizing, so that the same mistakes were made the second time around. Little was learned about downsizing in particular, or about responding to the economic cycle in general. Many organizations (e.g. BT, BP, British Gas) found that they had insufficient people left to take the business forward after recession.

- Management fads succeeded one another with bewildering speed, the next one arriving as soon as the previous one failed to produce immediate bottom-line benefits.

CAREERS AS TRANSITIONS

If organizations' strategic activity can be described as a series of transitions, so also can individuals' careers. Rather than a strategically planned set of building blocks completing a final imposing career edifice, careers, like organizational strategies, are emergent in an ever-changing context.

We challenge readers to look back at the major transitions in their career history and solemnly swear that they were all the fulfilment of plans rather than the seizing of opportunities or accepting an offer that could not be refused. With individuals' careers as with organizational activities, transitions occur at different levels:

- People can move from organizational to self-employment or un-employment.

- They can start working part time instead of full time.

- They can change one occupation or functional specialization for anoth-er, or they can become a generalist manager rather than a functional specialist.

- They can work in a different sector, in a different country, for another organization, or for two or more organizations instead of one.

- They can be promoted or demoted within the same organization, or they can simply move sideways to a different but similar job.

- They may have their role enlarged or changed because of others being made redundant.

- They can change their role's contents or even its objectives within the same job.

- They can move from one project team to another

- They can stay in the same role, but become a survivor of downsizing.

- And they can be involved in transitions at just one of these levels of analysis, or at several simultaneously.[11]

As with organizational transitions, so career transitions can be seen as proactive and one's own decision; as proactive and anticipating someone else's decision or the inevitable; or as reactive and involuntary. Just as a new organizational transition can start while the previous one is still in progress, so individuals can start preparing for their next role while they are still adjusting to the present one. As with opportunities and threats in organizational transitions, so individuals can identify supports and blocks to transitional success. And just as the success or failure of the higher levels of organizational transition can signal survival or catastro-phe, so the more profound career transitions can be crucial to an individ-ual's life and identity.

It is hardly surprising that continuous transitional change characterizes individual careers if it also constitutes the fundamental element of organizational activity. If structural changes such as takeovers and mergers, downsizings and outsourcings, are frequent events, then individuals' careers will be transformed as the new organizational form takes shape. As a manager from the organization taken over in a recent merger described, it is like having your entire cv erased and having to start again from scratch – on probation once more. But the central point of our argument is that transitions at the organizational and at the individual level follow the same sequence of phases. We therefore need to examine further the nature of preparation, encounter, adjustment and stabilization.

TRANSITIONAL PHASES

Preparation implies some degree of anticipation and proactivity. It requires getting one's mind around what seems to be going on and constructing a picture of a possible future way forward on that basis. Preparation therefore involves advance information: getting it, sharing it, and making some sort of sense and meaning out of it. **Encounter** is when messy reality intrudes upon that meaning; it is when the new information which we derive from experiencing what we prepared for forces us to revise our original ideas. The expectation–reality gap may be so wide that we are shocked that we could have been so wrong; or it could confirm most and contradict only a few of our expectations. But the information from the encounter phase is again vital, for it facilitates the next phase: **adjustment**. It is only when we are clear about the expectation–reality gap that we can adjust ourselves to the situation, or the situation to us. How far we will move in each of these two directions is a matter for negotiation. What we do know is that successful adjustment is highly satisfying, perhaps because we value a degree of congruence between ourselves and our environment.[12] Stabilization, the final phase, implies a steadier state, the outcome of the transition. It allows a degree of monitoring of the benefits and costs of the transition, since feedback will become available as its results work themselves through.

The reality of the transition cycle

Many will argue that today this is an idealized and prescriptive view of transitions. Totally unpredictable external events make it impossible to prepare, only to react. And the rate of organizational and career change is such that the stabilization phase is a figment of the imagination, an echo from the distant past. Its absence means that organizations and individuals have no feedback to inform them whether the transition has been successful and worthwhile. Hence the real transition cycle of today is truncated: it has only two phases, encounter and adjustment. Indeed, for some, encounter is the only reality: they merely lurch in a state of shell-shock from one emergency to the next.

All this is probably just an argument about words, however. Any response to an external event, however unpredictable, is still going to require some preparation. The brief preparation phase possible, however, is likely to prove an unsatisfactory basis for the following phases, and there is a lower probability of a successful transition. Similarly, even when a stabilization phase does not happen, there is still feedback possible about the success of the previous phase, adjustment. Indeed, it is arguable that this is the most important form of feedback, since it demonstrates degree of success in the process of changing, rather than the costs and benefits of the final post-transitional state. If change and transition are continuous, then it is the process and direction of those changes that need monitoring and evaluating, not the organization's state at any one moment in time. 'Now that we've got there, let's see how we're doing' is an unlikely proposal to hear in today's boardrooms.

DrugCo

Consider a pharmaceutical company. It recognized rapidly the implications of bio-technology for its research and development function. In the past, the development of new drugs required very large-scale facilities, partly because of the large number of compounds that had to be made and tested. However, the organization realized that bio-technology would permit much smaller scale and discrete R&D projects. It prepared, therefore, to save costs by contracting out much of the work to university departments.

When this transfer of work started in earnest, however, the company realized that the differences between the university research teams and their own R&D function were greater than they had anticipated. There were, for example, very different value priorities in the two cultures, with the university teams sometimes following promis-

ing side issues to the detriment of delivery dates for the contracted outcome. The company adjusted by rapidly training company
contract managers to liaise with the university contractors.

It also quickly realized that the redeployment of some of its
own R&D scientists into operational or marketing roles was not
proceeding satisfactorily, and developed a policy for outplacement of some and retraining of others. Competitive advantage
was now coming more from manufacturing speed and efficiency
and from global marketing, and less from the innovative nature of
the drugs themselves. So this company was managing well a
series of related transitions by anticipating or reacting quickly to
its environment, even though it had little chance to wait and see
how things were working out.

Sad Technograds

The most commonly quoted individual transition at work is that from
education to the world of work. Opportunities to get work experience
or reliable information are not often available or accessible. Instead,
false expectations are aroused, for example by glossy graduate
recruitment brochures. Research[13][14] has shown that commercially
oriented graduates increased their own preferences for growth and
rewards as they found over time that the organizational reality, while
not matching up to the promises, was not a million miles away. In
other words, they adjusted to the reality.

Technical graduates, on the other hand, did not in general get the
opportunities for analytic work that they expected and wanted. They,
however, did not adjust appropriately, since they actually increased
their preference for analytic work despite being unlikely to get it.
They reported lower psychological adjustment than their commer-
cial counterparts. Some of these technical graduates did not make
a satisfactory transition into the world of work at all, having failed to
adjust themselves to their roles or their roles to themselves. Their
job satisfaction was low.

'DrugCo' and 'Sad Technograds' are two examples of processes of truncated transition, where a new transition has to be started while the previ-

ous one is still running its course. The first is successful and organizational, the second is individual and often a mess.

In this chapter, then, we have argued that modern organizations are always in the process of transition. This is occurring at several different levels of analysis. The reason why transition is a constant is that the process of transition is always truncated: the final phase of transition, that of stabilization, seldom occurs. This is because the changes in the economic, business and technological environments are so rapid that there is no time for the adjusting organizational transition to be completed before the next necessary transition commences. As a result, the individual career transitions which are a necessary consequence of the organizational ones are also truncated, since they too are ever more frequent.

In the next chapter we examine the nature of organizational transitions. What do organizations change from and to, and what are the implications for individuals' careers? We believe that a full and realistic analysis of the context of organizational careers is necessary before we can start making recommendations regarding their management. As Slocum would doubtless have said, trying to understand what the elements are doing to your ship helps you plot your course and prevents you being tossed on the waves of managerial fashions and fads. Analysis does not necessarily lead to paralysis.

Some questions to think about

1. Does your organization claim to engage in strategic planning? How far ahead? To what extent are these original plans subsequently adhered to? Is there a mechanism for adapting them to changing circumstances? Is progress towards achievement assessed? Whose advice feeds into strategy-making? How aware are employees of the nature and success of strategic plans?

2. Think of a recent major transition undertaken by your organization. Was it prepared for adequately? How well was the actual encounter with the new state of affairs managed? How well did the organization adjust to the transition and how long did it take to do so? Was there a stabilization period, or was the next transition already underway?

3. Can you think of a major recent transition in your own career? Ask the same questions as in Question 2 about its phases. Can you see any connection between your own career transition and business transitions being undertaken by the organization? Are the two transitions congruent with one another?

REFERENCES

1 Mintzberg, H. (1987) 'Crafting strategy'. *Harvard Business Review* 65 (4): 65–75.
2 Miles, R.E. and Snow, C.C. (1978) *Organizational Strategy, Structure, and Process.* New York: McGraw-Hill.
3 Sonnenfeld, J.A. and Peiperl, M.A. (1988) 'Staffing policy as a strategic response: a typology of career systems'. *Academy of Management Review* 13: 588–600.
4 Legge, K. (1995) *Human Resource Management: Rhetorics and Realities.* London: Macmillan.
5 Weick, K.E. (1995) *Sensemaking in Organizations.* Thousand Oaks, CA: Sage.
6 Kay, J. (1993) *Foundations of Corporate Success.* Oxford: Oxford University Press.
7 Hamel, G. and Prahalad, C.K. (1994) *Competing for the Future.* Boston, MA: Harvard Business School Press.
8 Burgoyne, J., Pedler, M. and Boydell, T. (1994) *Towards the Learning Company.* Maidenhead: McGraw-Hill.
9 Nicholson, N. and West, M.A. (1988) *Managerial Job Change: Men and Women in Transition.* Cambridge: Cambridge University Press.
10 Nicholson, N. and West, M.A. (1989) 'Transitions, work histories, and careers', in M.B. Arthur, D.T. Hall, and B.S. Lawrence (eds) *Handbook of Career Theory.* Cambridge: Cambridge University Press.
11 Nicholson, N. and West, M.A. (1988) *Managerial Job Change: Men and Women in Transition.* Cambridge: Cambridge University Press.
12 Kohn, M.L. and Schooler, C. (1983) *Work and Personality.* Norwood, NJ: Ablex.
13 Nicholson, N. and Arnold, J. (1991) 'From expectation to experience: graduates entering a large corporation'. *Journal of Organisational Behaviour* 12: 423–9.
14 Keenan, A. and Newton, T.J. (1986) 'Work aspirations and experiences of young graduate engineers'. *Journal of Management Studies* 23: 224–37.

Keeping on course $\qquad$ 5

ORGANIZATIONAL CHANGE: CATACLYSM OR CONTINUUM?

What is the real nature of organizational transition? There are two fundamentally different accounts. One comes from the **cataclysmics**, the 'apocalypse now' camp. It suggests that organizations are currently transforming themselves into entirely new forms. Latching as they always do onto our preference for thinking in metaphors and opposites, the cataclysmics seek to persuade us that mechanisms are being transformed into networks, Fords into Microsofts.

The argument here is that technological change and other environmental cataclysms are forcing all organizations to change in the same direction or perish. Given this assumption, it becomes possible to hold up certain organizations as already transformed benchmarks for others to follow. If your business is to survive, runs the argument, you must become like ABB or Toyota or whoever is the current darling of the management press.[1]

And that means your HR practices too. ABB is very decentralized indeed, so local line management must be responsible for HR policies and practices. Lean and flexible means both contracting out and varied employment contracts, we are told; so we all need to segment out our employees into the favoured few at the core and the rest (who should be urged towards self-development). Promotion and security are gone for ever: concentrate on learning and employability. And for goodness' sake do not encourage people to be specialists; everyone has to be a general business person today.

The second perspective is much more cynical and less hyped. It is that of the **continuity** camp. All these things are cyclical, they suggest: we have seen it all before. Economic boom and bust are always accompanied by organizational growth and contraction, as night follows day. And HR policies and practices trail along behind like dachshunds, pumping their little legs as they try to keep up with their masters. As each economic downturn arrives, long-term development programmes turn into short-term training or just sitting next to Nellie; appraisal now means checking up on whether you have done what you were told, not discovering your development needs.

The dilemma for organizational change

So should we be camp followers? Should we side with the cataclysmics or the continuity camp? Each has its attractions. Admittedly, the cataclysmics urge us on to radical and revolutionary change, but at least they tell us what that change should be. All we have to do is follow the new best practice and we will get there. Agreed it will be painful, but then there is no gain without pain (or whatever other condescending catchphrase is in fashion). Whether the gain comes to us or to the change consultants is another question.

Or should we sink into the slough of despond with the continuity camp? No sooner have we established a decent graduate recruitment scheme than along comes the next recession and we give up on it. Oh well, at least we can put it in the drawer and dust it down when things get better again. So there seems to be a frustrating predictability about the cycle: plus ça change, plus c'est la même chose. We have seen it all before, so spare us the rhetoric. It feels like being a yo-yo on the end of a piece of string, but at least we are still yo-yos. We are glad we are not being asked to become electronic Martians by next Christmas.

There is indeed a lot of support from organizational analysts for the continuity position. They express it not in terms of recurring cycles, however, but rather as a series of dilemmas, of polar opposites between which organizations have to strike a balance. So for Richard Pascale,[2] the balances are between opportunism and planning, pluralism and elitism, discretion and mandate, transformation and management, individuality and collegiality, soft hearts and hard minds and metamizing versus maximizing skills (by which he means going beyond core competencies versus getting better at them). The first elements of all of Pascale's dilemmas tends towards under-control of the organization, the second towards over-control.

Or consider Charles Hampden-Turner's[3] list: autonomy versus interdependence, planning versus emergent strategy, low cost versus added value, mass market versus niche market, cash cows versus stars, straight technology versus the design of systems to suit people too, unfettered market versus equity, and cooperative or conflictual relations with other organizations.

Dilemma and transition

What both these authors are saying is that at any one point in time, an organization is likely to be on the move with respect to some or all of these dilemmas. It is likely to be in transition, perhaps moving further away from its ideal balance or perhaps towards it. Much of the change in organizations is thus to be seen in terms of seeking to achieve a balance along dimensions which are always going to be present in any medium-sized or large organization. Moreover, there will always be adjustments and readjustments occurring, since external changes such as the economic cycle will force them. Some organizations will have a good adjustment process, so that transitions are relatively minor movements to retain balance. Others have to make major transitions; their degree of imbalance is large, perhaps, for example, because a new CEO has just forced through a major change which is more in tune with his or her own philosophy than with the organization's environment.

So, as far as the continuity camp is concerned, there are some eternal verities that we ignore at our peril. The resolution of each of the dilemmas, the point of balance along each of the dimensions, will vary by organization, sector, point in the economic cycle, and so on. But resolution and balance there must be. The cataclysmics can rant on about tele-working and virtual organizations and so on, but the key dilemmas still remain. It is still an issue how much control you seek to exercise over teleworkers, for example, even though that control is exercised by systems rather than face to face.

Meanwhile the cataclysmics berate the continuity camp for ignoring the big picture. Unwilling to deal in such commonplaces as the economic cycle, they evoke Kondratieff Cycles from their intellectual armoury to persuade us that there are more fundamental changes afoot. We are in the throes of the information revolution, they assert, an upheaval of the same order of magnitude as the Industrial Revolution.[4] Corresponding upheavals in the nature of the employment relationship are only to be expected. As Charles Handy[5] puts it, organizations are for organizing work now, they are not for employing people.

Of course, these are caricatures of the continuity and the cataclysmic camps. Both of them do offer workable models to guide top management, and many have found them useful in responding to their business situation. What is unfortunate is that they are presented as mutually exclusive.

BLOWN OFF COURSE

As ever, Joshua Slocum provides the reconciliation of the two positions.
He recognizes the alternating phases of the sea, the soft and gentle breezes
replaced suddenly by the angry surge. Indeed, he prides himself on spot-
ting the signs of the weather's transformation a little in advance. He leaps
up from having a nice little sleep down in the cabin, where he had been
leaving *Spray* to steer herself or dreaming of a phantom crew doing it for
him. Racing up to the tiller, he lashes himself to it and guides the ship
over every wave and through every trough. He knows from long experience how the weather can change in an instant – which is as long as it
takes Wall Street to crash.

He also recognizes patterns in his own behaviour. Sometimes his eyes
are on the horizon, imagining what he will find when he gets there; he
checks up from his charts what he is expecting to find, and remembers
that in the end he is aiming for New England and home. Often, though,
he looks over the sides of the ship. Sometimes his eyes light upon tropical islands, with trees groaning with fruit and rows of local ladies sway-
ing their hips rhythmically in welcome. And this is not a dream.

Yet he dimly senses something more. A steamer, unlike the *Spray*, sticks
to its course regardless of the storms it encounters. People in his ports of
call know when he will arrive before he himself knows. Things will never
be the same as in the old days of sail and pigeon post. There are bigger
changes afoot, and their consequences are unclear.

The elements for keeping on course

We propose a model of organizational change that recognizes both perspectives, continuity and cataclysmic. First, there are three fundamental
elements to keeping on course:

- growth versus contraction
- long- versus short-termism
- centralization or devolution of decisions.

These three issues of size, perspective, and control are fundamental to business survival. We daily see organizations desperately addressing one or more
of them in their bid to survive. Takeovers, downsizings, divestments, alliances, forward planning, corporate culture programmes, and the scattering
of corporate HR are all signals that these issues are of paramount concern.

But the whole ocean is changing too. All the old ways of the sea are being overturned, and so the diversions off course come ever faster upon the organizational sailor. No sooner has he started adapting to a growth phase than contraction is upon him once more. No sooner has he acquired a portfolio of immediately profitable businesses or products than he has to prune them down to those which require his core competences only. No sooner has he bestowed a degree of autonomy to his international subsidiaries than he grabs it back with a gasp of relief. Great sea changes in markets, technology and competition force these changes of tack; it is so much harder these days to stay on course, and it looks like getting harder still. Small wonder that almost masochistically, some organizations inflict even more changes on themselves because others are engaging in them too – safety in numbers.

Just as organizations make continuous transitions between growth and contraction, long- and short-termism, and centralization versus devolution, so their HR policies and practices change accordingly. And as these organizational transitions follow one another ever more rapidly, so the HR function has greater and greater difficulty in keeping up with the rate of change and in providing appropriate services.

GROWTH AND CONTRACTION

First, then, the **growth versus contraction** dimension. The economic cycle is only one of the several determinants of this dimension. The nature and degree of the competition, the age, size, and sector of the organization, and the level of technological change, are others. As a consequence, although many organizations may be contracting simultaneously in the bust phase of the economic cycle, others will at the same time be in growth mode. Moreover, within some large organizations (for example, in the upstream and downstream businesses of Shell, differently affected by the price of oil) both expansion and contraction may be occurring simultaneously.

While contraction always seems to involve numerical contraction of the workforce, growth does not imply its expansion. Growth in terms of financial assets, turnover, and profit does not necessarily mean a corresponding growth in human assets. On the contrary, the usual aim is to cut costs, enhance productivity, and extract innovation with the same numbers of staff as before, or even from fewer (BT, for example). While the number of jobs advertised in the national press has increased steadily over the last few years, this increase has been more in small and medium than in large organizations.[6]

So if an organization's growth phase is primarily **organic** in nature, we will see higher productivity and more innovation expected from the existing workforce, or from a workforce of the same size. If growth is by **acquisition**, then while overall corporate numbers will increase, the total headcount in the now merged companies will be lower than it was before the acquisition. The conclusion is inescapable. Whether large organizations are in growth or contraction phase, more will be expected from, at most, the same numbers (growth), or from definitely fewer (contraction).

The question is: more of what? Growth is likely to involve moving into new markets with new products or services; it will normally require innovation and entrepreneurship. Contraction demands yet tighter control over costs, and higher productivity. We have already described this strategic dilemma in Chapter 1. Innovation requires autonomy, a sense of agency, the security to take reasonable risks, and teamworking.[7] Recent efforts at cost control have usually resulted in the erosion of these very conditions.[8]

The dilemma of transition

But the real dilemma is not that of choosing between growth and contraction. That is relatively clearcut and a matter of timing. It is, rather, how to make the transition from one to the other; for that transition will surely come. Very different sorts of skills and attitudes are required for cost control and enhanced productivity from those required for innovation and improved quality. And this requirement applies from the very top of the company down. Does this imply the need for wholesale dismissal of one sort of employee and recruitment of another? Should we segment the workforce, so that cuts are carried out on the periphery when cost control is at a premium, and resources are put into the core when we want more innovation? Or are there some just-in-time HR measures we can use to ensure that organizational transitions are accompanied by career transitions which match them?

LONG- VERSUS SHORT-TERMISM

What of the second transition: that between **long- and short-termism**? It is tempting to subsume this transition under that of growth and contractio. After all, we can only take the longer view when we can afford to do so, goes the argument. Yet a moment's reflection suggests that sometimes the opposite holds. Consider, for example, the emphasis placed on 'sticking to the knitting' during the recession of the early 1990s. Company after company tried to decide what its core competencies were, what few things it did so well that they gained it competitive advantage, and then jettison everything else. For every Hanson or BAT acquiring and divesting businesses in a variety of sectors, there was an ICI or a GrandMetropolitan defining down their business. In ICI's case this involved demerger, in GrandMet's the redefinition of the business as the acquisition and management of food and drink brands.

So the distinction here is between opportunistic moves into and out of markets, when the tropical island may produce quick fruit or may turn out to be a snare and a delusion, versus a focus on one or two core competences and a clear vision of where one is going in the longer term, with the concomitant risk of putting all one's eggs into one or two baskets. Or, perhaps more often, the dilemma is between seeking to cut costs now and impress the stockmarkets versus investing in research and development over the longer term to ensure future profitability. Many business people perceive this to be no choice at all; if they do not please the analysts and investors in the short term, there will be no long term to invest in.[9]

Implications of the dilemma

Once again, the two alternatives, long-term focus and short-term opportunism, both have very different people implications. Sudden excursions into new markets or products require new knowledge and skills which are unlikely to have been developed internally. Hiring and firing rather than training and development are the order of the day. What training is provided has as its objective the improvement of performance on a particular job, or the acquisition of a newly required skill. Performance improvement, not the development of potential, becomes the main concern. People get taken on to do a job, and the deal is a very instrumental and transactional one; there is little of a relationship to be developed. While the core competencies for the future require the long-term development of specialist skills, all that opportunism needs is flexibility: the ability to acquire and exercise new skills as and when required. Long term means investing in people; short term means buying them in.

And once again, the problem is not so much how to manage careers, whether you are taking a short-term business perspective or a long-term one. Text books are full of the systems and processes required in each case.

Long-termers

Long-termers favour:

- HR resourcing plans to match strategic business directions
- succession plans
- development centres and career workshops
- appraisal to ascertain development needs

and similar aspects of organizational management.

Short-termers

Short-termers are on the ball in terms of:

- their knowledge of their labour markets and how to recruit the people they need
- getting them up to speed in the shortest time possible
- maximizing their performance by incentives
- making as explicit as possible what it is they want from them in return.

The real dilemma, though, is not so much how best to manage in short-term or in long-term mode. It is rather how to make the transition from one to the other. How do you start investing in people when you have only hired and fired them for the last five years? Conversely, how do you bring in new blood when people have been there all their working lives? Again, provided the will and the resources are there, it is not hard to discover what you need to do when you are tacking in one direction rather than the other. The transition between the two is the difficulty, when the boom comes across and thwacks you firmly on the back of the head. We only need to reflect on recent cases, where companies noted for their long-termism lurched temporarily into the opposite phase, to see the dangers of this strategic transition. Marks and Spencer and Price Waterhouse both disrupted or postponed a year's graduate intake some years ago, and both may still be feeling the consequences.

CENTRALIZATION VS DEVOLUTION

The final change of tack is that between centralization and devolution. In recent years devolution has more often been preached than practised,[10] and here too there are contradictions galore. Empowerment to take local decisions for speed and quality's sakes is snatched back when central financial controls are so tight as to remove all but the cheapest option. 'Here are your targets; it's up to you how you choose to reach them' is often a cruel deceit. At one extreme we have tiny corporate centres, containing only those services to the businesses which have to be corporate in order to achieve economies of scale or for legal reasons; legal services, corporate communications, and the chief executive's office are examples. In such organizations, corporate HR has been stripped down to a pale shadow of its former self (WH Smith has reduced corporate HR from 47 people to 6[11]). At the other extreme we have a powerful HR presence at the corporate centre, strategic planners, a large centralized finance function, and a strongly national central focus for a multinational organization.

Devolved career management

Devolved career management is the responsibility of local line managers. They are expected to:

- help their subordinates to develop so that they benefit the business and the corporation

- ignore the benefits that their best people bring to their own bonuses if they retain them in their own unit

- encourage subordinates to develop themselves, perhaps using personal development plans or learning centres.

However, operational demands may often take precedence during time at work,[12] and managerial reward systems which use the degree of development of subordinates as a criterion are thin on the ground. Furthermore, line managers may simply lack the skills and knowledge required for the task. Devolved HR professionals may be on hand to help, but they are often fully occupied in trying to ensure that minimal standards in HR practices are adhered to. Or else they themselves are trying to develop and execute policy.

The Civil Service

Devolution has had a profound effect on careers in the UK Civil Service. One of the attractions of the Civil Service was the potential career variety it offered. Although in practice most employees did not move between major departments, some did, and so the possibility of roving across the service was part of the culture. Devolution has led not only to a divergence of personnel practices between departments. The further fragmentation through the creation of agencies and the geographical dispersal of the Civil Service has made the career domain across which employees can travel very much smaller. From the individual's point of view this has obviously reduced career options. From the organizational perspective, it has reduced the capacity to respond to change by redeployment. Thus the positive benefits of increased business focus brought about by devolution are at least partly offset by career frustration among staff.

Centralized career management

By the same token, more centralized career management also has its problems. A fast-track graduate stream may soon lose many of its members in an age of decreasing organizational commitment. And a corporate pool of 200 from whom the board will be drawn can consume a major share of development resources and cause feelings of inequity in others. Nevertheless, centralized management of careers has a range of well-tried methods at its disposal.

But, as with the other two dilemmas, it is not one tack or the other that is the real issue. It is rather the transition between the two, the changing of tack, when the centre feels the need to reassert control, or when sudden diversification or expansion makes increased devolution an attractive solution. Both the surrender of control and its grabbing back are fraught with difficulties, yet they are happening all the time.

SEA CHANGES

But what of the sea changes? What of those huge social, economic, political and technological changes that form the context of career management? How far can we take the cataclysmics' argument that these are already revolutionizing the nature of the employment relationship, and career management with it? Ignoring the wilder shores of fantasy, many argue that we are witnessing a change in the three points of balance of organizations. The balance is moving from growth to contraction, from long to short term, and from centralization to devolution, they assert.[13]

Yet such a view is highly culture specific.[14] The origins of management ideas are very strongly American, where the historical background is indeed of large bureaucratic manufacturing organizations giving way to entrepreneurial knowledge-based service organizations. But there is a wide range of organizations in the western world, including, for example, assembly plants for Japanese automobiles or Korean microchips which import wholesale the HR practices of their countries of origin. Moreover, the changes in balance that are alleged to be universal are unlikely to apply to smaller organizations, in which nearly half of the working population is now employed.

And it is altogether too pat to assume that information technology will be the tool for devolving decisions. When we consider the uses to which IT is being put in the developing service sector, we can see its countervailing attractions as a means of control. Consider, for example, the nature of telesales and customer complaint handling systems.[15] The technology enables supervisors to monitor every feature of staff activity: speed of response, length of call, time away from phone, etc. The all-seeing eye is already with us.

A more cautious prediction is not about the overall **directions** of change. Rather, it is about the **frequency** of the three transitions. We will have to change tack more often. Given the exponential increases in knowledge and in its translation into techniques, goods and services, and given the increased speed of acquisition of that knowledge and its applications worldwide, then the one thing that we can conclude with complete confidence is that the rate of change in the environment will continue to increase. This means that organizations will need to make more frequent anticipatory or reactive adjustments to these changes. Transitions will become yet more frequent. Even in the best-run companies, where the diversion from the course set is small (e.g. Marks and Spencer, Unilever), the frequency of transitions is increasing. This drives organizations to seek appropriate structural responses. They go for project or matrix structures in order to gain flexibility of response, and find themselves decentralizing willy-nilly as a consequence.

JUST-IN-TIME CAREER MANAGEMENT

The conclusion is inescapable: just-in-time (JIT) career management will become the norm. There are many career management approaches which assume that a consistent balance is always there, and that it is located towards the growth, long-term and centralized tacks. There are others that refuse to contemplate any organizational involvement whatever; they are located towards the contraction, short-term and devolved tacks at present. Both seem to believe that that is where they will always be. Neither approach is likely to be right for long. For the ship will move on, and what is right for one tack will be inappropriate for the next. Given the cost in time and money to set up a Rolls Royce of a graduate training programme, for example, it is costly indeed to abandon it when there is no money to support it or when there are no jobs for the graduates to go to. Rather, the need will be for career interventions the purposes of which are:

• to help individuals make the transitions which the business needs them to make

• to make them fast enough to coincide in time with the business transition itself.

The task facing JIT processes

So how will organizations seek to manage careers so that they get 'the right people in the right place at the right time'? This is indeed a hard task when we recall that whatever they do will have to meet the needs of the business in both the growth and the contraction tacks; and it will have to be capable of moving across quickly and cheaply from one to the other tack. So too with the short- versus long-term, and the centralization versus devolution diversions; in all three cases, organizations will need just-in-time processes which support the business in either tack and in its transitions from one to the other. When we consider how difficult some of these transitions are, e.g. from a short- to a longer term perspective, or from expansion to contraction, the true enormity of the career management task becomes clear.

But the greatest challenge of all is to manage these career transitions when the mutual trust and support needed to make them successfully are in such scarce supply.

To recapitulate the argument of the first five chapters (Part I of this book):

- The amount of social capital available in western societies is decreasing, and with it the degree of trust (Chapter 1).

- The recent actions of organizations in response to environmental pressures have further decreased trust (Chapter 2).

- Insecurity regarding jobs and other features of the employment situation has added to this effect (Chapter 3).

- Organizations' response to the increase in the speed of environmental change is to engage in ever more frequent transitions (Chapter 4).

- These business transitions are cyclical in nature, and imply corresponding individual career transitions (Chapter 5).

- Trust is a necessary condition for such career transitions to be made successfully, yet it is in exceedingly short supply.

Some questions to think about

1. Is your organization currently in a growth or a contraction phase? Long- or short-term perspective? Centralizing or devolving? Can you make these generalizations of the whole organization, or are different businesses at different phases? Has your organization/business recently entered the phase it is now in, or has it had a long and uninterrupted history of being on this tack? Do you detect any hints of a change of tack? What such hints might you be looking for? How soon do you think any such change of tack will occur? What might precipitate it?

2. Think back to the most recent change of tack that you can recall. What were its HR implications? Were they foreseen and planned for, or dealt with reactively? What were the consequences of how the HR issues were addressed?

3. Have you ever been involved in a merger or takeover? Were you in the taking over or the taken over organization? How were the HR implications of the takeover dealt with? How did it feel to be taking or taken over? What were the consequences of this organizational transition for your own career transitions? Were these consequences necessary and desirable for the organization? For you?

REFERENCES

1 Herriot, P. and Pemberton, C. (1995) *New Deals: The Revolution in Managerial Careers.* Chichester: Wiley.
2 Pascale, R. (1990) *Managing on the Edge.* New York: Simon & Schuster.
3 Hampden-Turner, C. (1990) *Charting the Corporate Mind.* Oxford: Blackwell.
4 Scott Morton, M.S. (1991) *The Corporation of the 1990s.* New York: Oxford University Press.
5 Handy, C. (1994) *The Empty Raincoat.* London: Hutchinson.
6 MSL Index (1994–7). London: MSL International.
7 West, M.A. and Farr, J.L. (1990) *Innovation and Creativity at Work: Psychological and Organisational Strategies.* Chichester: Wiley.
8 Herriot, P. and Pemberton, C. (1995) *New Deals: The Revolution in Managerial Careers.* Chichester: Wiley.
9 Hutton, W. (1994) *The State We're In.* London: Jonathan Cape.
10 Legge, K. (1995) *Human Resource Management: Rhetorics and Realities.* London: Macmillan.
11 Tamkin, P., Barber, L. and Hirsh, W. (1995) 'Personal development plans: case studies of practice'. Brighton: Institute for Employment Studies, Report 280.
12 Hamel, G. and Prahalad, C.K. (1994) *Competing for the Future.* Boston, MS: Harvard Business School Press.
13 Sparrow, P.R. (1996) 'Careers and the psychological contract: understanding the European context'. *European Journal of Work and Organisational Psychology* 5 (4): 479–500.
14 Arkin, A. (1997) 'Hold the production line'. *People Management* 3 (3): 22–7.
15 Hendry, C. and Pettigrew, A. (1990) 'Human resource management: an agenda for the 1990s'. *International Journal of Human Resource Management* 1 (1): 17–44.

PART II

Changing course

Introduction

TRUST AND TRANSITIONS: THE IMPLICATIONS

If we take seriously the analysis of Part I, then there are some radical implications to be drawn about how careers should be managed. First, if trust is a necessary condition for the employment relationship, and if trust has been lost, then it follows that the first priority is to restore it. And second, if the essential element of careers is transitions rather than jobs, then the central tasks of career management are to enable both individuals and organizations to choose those transitions which meet their needs and to make them successfully. The second part of the book seeks to relate these two implications to each other. We will argue that only if trust is restored is it possible to make transitions successfully; and that negotiating transitions is itself one way of restoring trust.

The restoration of trust is best accomplished by top management demonstrating by its actions that it habitually does what it says it is going to do. As we argued at the end of Chapter 3, this will require it to be miserly with promises and to eschew rhetoric. The restoration of trust will also necessitate acting by the same principles as it expects from its employees. This includes being as efficient and effective at its own job as it urges subordinates to be at theirs. Above all, it must be seen to exercise the power of its position in the organization's interests and those of the stakeholders rather than in its own.

Of course, the restoration of trust is not solely the responsibility of top management. Trust is mutual and reciprocal, and employees need to show that they too can be trusted, once given the opportunity to demonstrate the fact. It is the responsibility of top management to ensure that they are given this opportunity, however, by loosening up on control. We therefore feel justified in laying the task of restoring trust on top management's shoulders in the first instance.

Their present business situation provides organizations with a tremendous challenge in terms of trust. For the necessity of transition at the organizational and the individual level requires the exercise of trust both in and by top management. Consider first the business transitions. How can top management persuade people that sudden growth from a hitherto static position is the right change to make? How can they possibly justify the surrender of long-term agreed plans for a short-term opportunity? How can they argue for the sudden withdrawal of corporate support in the name of devolution to the businesses? The answer is: not without huge difficulties, and only if they enjoy a degree of trust in their judgement and motives.

But as we have argued, such business transitions as these inevitably imply individual career transitions. Yet the individuals involved will not necessarily perceive this inevitability. On the contrary, they will require persuading that the personal transitions they are being asked to make are really needed. And they will want it to be crystal clear that the processes whereby career transitions are inferred from organizational ones are equitable and transparent. Once again, it is unthinkable that such changes can be carried through successfully without a high degree of trust.

Yet, paradoxically, the current situation does not only desperately need the exercise of trust, it also provides a splendid opportunity for its restoration. For the only way in which career transitions can be successfully managed is by doing deals with employees such that the transitions they are asked to make meet some of their own needs as well as those of the organization. And the way in which deals are done, kept, and seen to be kept, can regenerate trust. The reason is that if deals are kept, the parties are seen to be doing what they said they would do. As we have emphasized throughout, keeping agreements is probably the biggest source of trust.

Of course, this is somewhat of a chicken and egg situation. Trust is needed if career deals are to be made and kept, but the making and the keeping will enhance the trust available. The trust chick is so fragile and vulnerable a creature, however, that unless certain principles are adhered to in the management of career transitions, we are convinced it will perish as soon as it emerges from its egg. Successful career management requires:

- a process of contracting between top management and employees as to which transitions are to be made and by whom, which takes account of individual differences in needs and motives

- a process of support for making transitions which ensures that the appropriate learning and development occurs

- a process of information exchange throughout these previous two processes

- the management of career transitions so that they mesh with business transitions

- organizational leadership which engenders trust and gives meaning to business and personal transitions.

The five chapters of Part II deal with these five requirements for successful career management. They are extremely demanding requirements for organizations to fulfil. We believe that they only stand a chance of achievement if organizations adopt some general principles about the nature of career management. 'Adopting' does not necessarily mean broadcasting them as yet another vision from above. Rather it means acting according to them, and explaining actions later when one has engendered enough trust for one's explanation to be believed. What are these general principles? We believe them to be relatively few in number, capable of being expressed in the process of career contracting[1][2] and capable of being presented in a simple process model.[3]

The general principles that will need to underpin the employment relationship of the future are:

- Top management and other employees do not necessarily have the same interests and needs; the HRM rhetoric is false.

- There is a wide variety of interests and needs among employees.

- Both the organization's needs as construed by top management and the needs of individual employees have to be met in the employment relationship.

- The process of agreeing the nature of the offers each party is willing and able to make in order to meet the needs of the other is best described as contracting.

- Career contracting relates to that part of this process which concerns the transitions which employees will make and how they will make them.

- Contracting and recontracting are continuous processes as the needs of both parties are constantly changing.

- By definition, a contract should not be imposed by either party merely because it has the power to do so. This is because the process of contracting itself enhances commitment to its outcomes, since both parties have given their assent.

In the second part of this book, we recommend career management policies, processes and practices which follow these principles. Chapter 6 describes the career contracting process in more detail. It explores the ways in which a reconciliation may be made between the needs of organizations for certain transitions by individuals, and the needs of those individuals, which may be met in some transitions but not in others. We emphasize the different needs felt by different individuals, and therefore the possibility in principle of such a reconciliation. In Chapter 7 we explore the sort of help that they will need in making transitions, emphasizing that any training and development must now be aimed at aiding transitions rather than preparing for jobs. In both these chapters, the different perspectives that top management and employees bring to the issues are made clear. One potential difficulty in contracting careers is removed when the differences between the parties' perspectives become clearer. In Chapter 8 we detail the information needs if the right choice of and successful passage through transitions are to happen. In Chapters 9 and 10 we review the managerial and the leadership tasks facing top management in particular if they are to manage careers so as to meet both the business and also the individual needs.

REFERENCES

1   Rousseau, D.M. (1995) *Psychological Contracts in Organizations*. Thousand Oaks, CA: Sage.
2   Herriot, P. and Pemberton, C. (1996) 'Contracting careers'. *Human Relations* 49 (6): 757–90.
3   Herriot, P. and Pemberton, C. (1997) 'Facilitating new deals'. *Human Resource Management Journal* 7 (1): 45–56.

Flexible friends 6

THE ORGANIZATION'S PERSPECTIVE

Our two key ideas so far in this book have been **transition** and **trust**. These ideas underpin the issue addressed in this chapter: how can organizations and individuals enhance their flexibility in ways which meet both parties' needs?

The parties approach the issue from two very different perspectives. For the organization, the different forms of flexibility offer a variety of business benefit.[1] Flexibility in the provision of labour means that labour supply can be meshed with its demand as smoothly as possible. This can be achieved by flexibility in terms both of the time when labour is available and also of contract terms. Costs can be reduced by having labour available only when it is needed. Part-time, fixed-term, shiftwork, or just zero-hour contracts where employees can be summoned when and if they are needed, are all methods of flexing labour provision.

Flexible working has increased in all phases of the economic cycle. Fixed-term and temporary contracts increase in number during growth as extra labour is required to enhance output. During recession, they allow uncertainty of demand to be managed. Meanwhile, the roles of those remaining in full-time employment are likely to be enlarged, and IT will reduce further the amount of work requiring people.[2]

Flexibility within and across roles also has its business benefits. If workforce and managers are multiskilled or multifunctional, they can be switched to areas of work where there is a temporary shortage of labour. They may even change function if there is a strategic shift in functions, for example, towards marketing and away from production. Or, having worked within a functional unit or department, people may be allocated to a project team in order to increase speed to market or create a necessary change. All of these transitions save both time and money – time in recruiting and induction to fill the new need, and money in redundancy and recruitment costs.

IBM

In the fast-moving computing world, having the right people in the right place at the right time is not only critical, it is also hard to achieve. Work tends to be carried out in projects of variable length. Lead times can be very short and specifications can alter quickly. Furthermore, the skills required are high level and technical, very specific to the task. IBM's UK laboratory copes with this problem through a fortnightly meeting of senior departmental managers. They look at the labour they have available, the work required to be completed, and the timescales within which it has to be done. With this information, they:

- juggle staff between projects

- transfer them between departments

- identify skill shortages and deal with them through training plans

- recognize skill surpluses and reskill, redeploy or at worst separate

- hire in temporary extra labour, or subcontract activities outside

- initiate new recruitment.

In making these judgements, IBM considers the relative importance and urgency of the projects, wider business imperatives, affordability, and planning and budgetary constraints. All this happens against a background of open advertising, where employees can present their credentials for work, and where a skills database composed by staff themselves is available to managers.

But role flexibility has another benefit too. The more such transitions individuals make, the better learners they are likely to become.[3] Hence organizational needs for innovation and change are more likely to be met.

The two flexibilities (of labour provision and of role) are therefore hugely attractive to organizations. For in principle they offer a means of solving their most pressing business dilemma: how to compete on cost but at the same time develop new and better products, services or inter-

nal processes. But flexibility does not only refer to having a larger proportion of the workforce on other than full-time regular contracts. It also
implies movement between tasks, roles, functions and formal employment contracts; it implies ever more frequent transitions.

Shell UK

Shell UK Exploration and Production has succeeded in achieving
contractual flexibility and flexibility across roles at the same time.
About one-third of staff is contracted-in agency and temporary staff,
another third contracted-out to allied contractors, and one-third is
full-time core staff. Yet even among the last, there is a high number
of job transitions. In any one year, 25 percent change jobs, and only
7 percent are promotions. Wastage is less than 3 percent per year.
Horizontal progression gives new challenges and learning opportunities, and in some areas there is considerable functional flexibility.

THE EMPLOYEE'S PERSPECTIVE

Which is where the second perspective comes in: that of the individual
employee. For each of these transitions has major implications for people.

Transitions from role to role, or project to project, whether these are
upwards or sideways, seem on balance to have beneficial effects on people. Yes, there is sometimes anxiety about their capacity to do the new job,
and yes, there may often be a great deal of ambiguity about what it is that
they are expected to do in it. But provided the resources are there, such
changes generally have positive psychological effects,[4] and staff have a
more favourable attitude towards the employment relationship as a result.[5]

When we move on to the more profound transitions the consequences
for individuals become more potentially threatening. Any role transition
which is a demotion, any involuntary move from a full-time to another
form of contract, any unexpected exit from the organization, is recognized to be a threat to one's lifestyle. Now lifestyle itself is a marketing
concept. It implies that we may make choices among a variety of ways of
using our time and money, but that none of them is likely to be personally damaging. Yet the reality is that any change in employment status
which decreases income may have profound effects upon an individual's
and their dependants' housing, pension, healthcare, education and overall welfare.[6] What is more, as we demonstrated in Chapter 3, the chances

of returning to a full-time job at the same or a higher level of remuneration after a period without one are very low indeed. We are talking survival and well-being here, not lifestyle.

Some transitions may also affect an individual's identity. Some examples are:

- A demotion will have a profound effect on someone whose identity is bound up with their organizational status.

- A cross-functional move may threaten an individual's professional or occupational identity; so may a move from a functional to a general management role.

- A move out of full-time work may impact upon one's perceived role as breadwinner of the family.[7]

- A move out of an organization may destroy any identification with that organization, possibly built up over a number of years.

- Any sideways, downwards or flexibility facing move may threaten one's career identity. By this we mean, for example, a threat to one's identity as someone who is upwardly mobile.[8]

- Any move is apt to make us regret that we have not yet fully reaped the benefits of the investment of ourselves and our knowledge and skills that we have put into our present role.[9]

Of course, not all transitions will have negative effects upon identity and self-esteem. A promotion, for example, or a role change or enlargement can enhance these elements of the self. So can a move out of the organization, when this is self-initiated or the result of being headhunted.

CAREER ANCHORS

Thus different transitions may have different implications. But also, those implications will be different for different individuals. There is any number of ways of looking at differences between individuals: personality, intelligence, interests, motivations, age, experience and so on. We have focused on one dimension of individual differences only, which is closely related to careers. It is that of career anchors. We each have a career anchor,[10] that element of our work which in the final analysis we would not give up. Eight such anchors have been identified, and their labels speak for themselves:

- security

- autonomy/independence

- technical/functional

- managerial

- entrepreneurship

- service/dedication

- pure challenge

- life-style integration.

Usually it is not too difficult to tease out an individual's career anchor, particularly with the help of Ed Schein's questionnaire.[10] However, for some it may be a close-run thing. Apart from his literal anchor, Joshua Slocum, for example, may have had two competing career anchors. Listen to his diary entries, the first for the day he sets out on his epic voyage, the second for the day he returns:

> My step was light on deck in the crisp air. I felt that there could be no turning back, and that I was engaging in an adventure the meaning of which I thoroughly understood. I had taken little advice from anyone, for I had a right to my own opinion in matters pertaining to the sea.

> I see, as I look back over my own small achievement, a kit of not too elaborate carpenter's tools, a tin clock, and some carpet tacks, to facilitate the enterprise as already mentioned in the story. But above all to be taken into account were some years of schooling, where I studied with diligence Neptune's laws, and these laws I tried to obey when I sailed overseas: it was worth the while.

Pure challenge? Or technical/functional?

Obviously, the impact of any given transition for a particular individual will partly depend on their primary career anchor:

- For those with a technical/functional anchor, cross-functional moves or moves into general management are likely to be particularly difficult.

- For managerial types, demotion or a sideways move which decreases one's number of subordinates or resources will be threatening.

- A transition to part or complete self-employment might attract those who value autonomy/independence or entrepreneurship.

- Frequent role changes will appeal to those who welcome pure challenge.

- A move to part-time work, provided it is secure, may well be attractive to those for whom lifestyle integration is their anchor.

- Those for whom security is a prime concern are only likely to welcome a transition if its perceived likely consequence is increased security.

So the ever-increasing frequency of transitions is not necessarily an unwelcome development for everyone. On the contrary, for some it represents a greater opportunity to realize their career anchor sooner than used to be possible in more predictable times. What we do not know, though, is the relative frequency of these anchors in the working population. The original theory was developed on business school graduates, and the subsequent data are derived from managerial and professional staff. They show, not surprisingly, that technical/functional and managerial are the most commonly held anchors by that population, although some recent data suggest that lifestyle integration is coming more to the fore, even for these groups.

The constant danger is that those who live to work project their own motivations onto the vast majority who work to live. A recent research project[11] demonstrated that a cross-section of the UK workforce was more preoccupied with the basic wage, work environment, and security aspects of the employment deal than was a sample of managers. For very many, the need to survive at above the poverty level makes career anchors merely academic. Even if they hanker after technical excellence or autonomy, security will be their major concern.

The conclusion has to run as follows: organizations need employees to engage in a variety of career transitions. Depending on the individual's motivation and circumstances, some of these transitions may be welcome for some individuals. However, given the likely preoccupation with security of many of them, especially those at the lower end of the organizational hierarchy, those transitions which threaten security are likely to be unpopular. There are therefore two tasks; the first is to discover and attempt to match career anchors and other individual needs to the transitions with which they are compatible; the second is to decrease the insecurity associated with most transitions. We initially examine a solution which at first sight appears radical enough to address these issues successfully. Its description here permits us to contrast the really radical nature of the process of career contracting which we believe to be necessary.

INPLACEMENT

The long-term costs of the most favoured transition of the last ten years – transition out of the organization – are now becoming apparent.[12] [13] [14] No long-term financial benefits of downsizing have been observed; commitment to the organization among those who remain has plummeted; so has security, a loss which in its turn reduces the conditions for innovation; and good employees have been lost to the organization. What are the alternatives? How can transitions and trust coexist?

One overall strategy aimed at achieving this reconciliation has been called '**Inplacement**'.[15] Its elements are as follows:

- All internal potential transitions are advertised, internally, and are placed in the context of the current business directions.

- Retraining and development opportunities are made available to those about to make a transition.

- Work is redesigned so as to use employees' knowledge and skills more effectively (for example, by the formation of an internal contingent workgroup of troubleshooters, available for any emergency).

- Security is added to non-full-time jobs (for example, by agreeing the same conditions for part-time as for full-time employees; by guaranteeing a renewal opportunity at the end of a fixed-term contract).

- Effective resource planning is carried out so that job losses may occur through natural wastage.

- A short period of part-time work, and temporary reductions in pay or a pay freeze for all (including top management) is undertaken in periods of contraction.

- Early retirement with the guarantee of a period of consultancy or part-time work becomes part of the programme (for example, NatWest's Employment Register and IBM's Skill Base).

Rover plc

Rover provides an example of an inplacement approach. An under-taking has been given (the 'New Deal') that no employee will suffer compulsory redundancy. In exchange for this added security, employees are expected to be entirely flexible in terms of the transi-tions they are prepared to make. So there are, for example, former white-collar workers at Rover who have made the transition to work-ing on the shopfloor. Despite a sequence of new owners (and new chief executives), Rover has achieved overall a steady improvement in employee morale and career satisfaction over the last few years. This is doubtless partly due to an increase in trust, as Rover has resolutely stuck to its side of the bargain throughout.

CAREER CONTRACTING AND ITS IMPLICATIONS

Commendable as such initiatives as Rover's are, however, we need to consider whether they fulfil both of the requirements we cited earlier. They certainly decrease insecurity, but do they match transitions to the needs and career anchors of different employees? Do they, in other words, fulfil the requirements of career contracting?

In essence, Rover's New Deal is flexibility for security. Yet as we have already argued, different people want and need different things. Rover was most probably correct in assuming that security was the greatest sin-gle concern overall of the workforce. It was able to rely on a recent indus-trial relations history in which the New Deal was embedded. Yet it might arguably have got a better deal for the employees and the organization if it had guaranteed security only for those whose career anchor it was. It also needs to attract and retain individuals with other career anchors: technical/functional, for example, or pure challenge, especially as BMW with its passion for engineering excellence is the new owner. And it is only if those anchors are addressed in the employment deal that the indi-viduals who hold them will be as motivated as they might be.

Process versus content

Other organizations have concentrated on the content of the deal in a far less benign way than has Rover. Ignoring employee diversity, such organizations rhetorically contrast the bad old deal of security for loyalty with the good and indeed inevitable new deal of employability for flexibility. Clearly, the rhetorical assumption of inevitability is used to justify the imposition of a single form of deal. The organization gets its flexibility alright, but all that the employees get in return is the dubious assurance that if they are flexible in the firm's interests now, they will be more employable later somewhere else. Give up your narrow professional expertise and become a thrusting general manager, they are urged. Who needs narrow-minded engineers or chemists? Increased flexibility within the organization may increase internal employability, but maybe only by adding to the individual's firm-specific knowledge which is not transferable. The persuasive rhetoric may have reduced rather than enhanced employability. No wonder that rhetoric and its authors are mistrusted.

Organizations need to concentrate more upon the process of career dealing than upon the contents of career deals.[16] For they need to discover the wants and offers of individuals or of groups of staff, to match them with their own wants and offers and to negotiate. The contracting process requires organizations to:

- infer not only which tack the business environment implies for the organization, but also social trends

- infer from the business environment which transitions they will be wanting employees to make and what they can offer in return

- infer from social trends which transitions employees are likely to be willing to make, and what they are able and willing to offer in return

- discover, by providing and eliciting information, whether employee offers are likely to match organization wants, and whether organizational offers are likely to match employee wants

- do this for individuals, or at the very least for groups of similar individuals, rather than for employees overall

- make offers accordingly, and negotiate a deal

- monitor it to discover whether it is still in accord with needs, whether it is equitable, and whether it is being kept

- renegotiate new deals if these conditions are not being met or if the business and social contexts require.

This process is represented in Figure 6.1.

The implications of contracting about transitions in this way are pro-

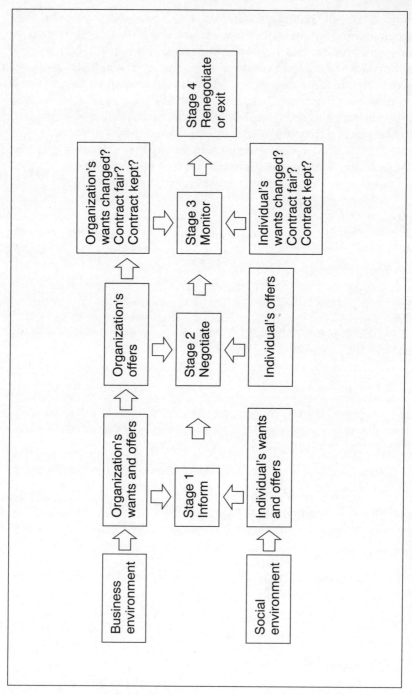

Figure 6.1 Contracting transitions

found.[17] The first and most obvious is that the **process is two-way**. Individuals make explicit for themselves and for the organization what their career anchors and circumstances are, and hence which transitions they are or are not willing to entertain and which they would positively welcome. The organization makes no prior assumptions about these preferences, it simply finds out what they are. The danger of projecting the live-to-work values of the senior managerial cadre onto the work-to-live values of much of the workforce is thus avoided. So is the risk of imposing a particular deal, however apparently fair and reasonable, onto employees when only some of them want it.

KEY POINT

Recent IES work in a public sector organization exemplifies this two-way element of career contracting. It addressed the career issues of the layer of staff just below senior management. Because of downsizing, these employees were less likely than in the past to get promoted, and so were staying for many years at the same level, and even in the same job. Yet they had joined the organization mainly for the career variety it offered. A close dialogue about the needs of this group and the organization led to a clear agenda for action which would assist lateral movement and ongoing skill development. It included clarification of varied career paths, for both generalists and specialists; the opportunity for career review interviews and career workshops; and improved management skills training.

The second implication of the career contracting model is that contracting is **iterative**. The organization may change tack with ever-increasing frequency, and thus regularly and repeatedly require a new set of transitions. But individuals' needs change too, as changed personal circumstances and cultural trends continuously impose new priorities. While career anchors are relatively stable over time, people are usually willing to go for a second best if needs must. So frequent iteration of the contracting process is likely to be necessary for both parties.

The third implication of the contracting model is that the deal becomes **more explicit** as well as more individualized. In organizations where the career deal was uniform across the organization it was assumed, for example, that everyone wanted promotional transitions, or that perks were as important as basic salary. Yet the desired deals are far more varied, and because the process of dealing is explicit, this variety can be taken into account and acted upon.

Flexibility versus segmentation

By the same token, the contracting model should not result in the simplistic and divisive segmentation typical of some of today's organizations.[18] In some such companies:

- Carefully planned and agreed job moves are the norm only for those singled out as of high potential.

- Professionals whose work is not core to the organization's mission are forced to become independent contractors.

- Middle managers are downsized or retained in the same job, and acquire the label deadwood.

- The full-time workforce is bought in, used up and spewed out.

- The contingent workforce is hired through agencies with as little managerial involvement as possible.

Under the contracting model this scenario could not occur, since it is inconceivable that all of the employees mentioned would have negotiated such a deal. The segmented organization has achieved its objective of flexibility, but at the cost of some employees' wants and needs.

HR PROCESSES FOR CAREER CONTRACTING

However, to engage in the career contracting process does require some additional processes besides those just described as necessary for a strategy of inplacement. First, consider the informing stage in Figure 6.1.

- Organizations need to be able to work out in advance what transitions the approaching changes of tack in business direction will require.

- They need to be aware of the range of transitions they could offer which are compatible with these requirements.

- They should be enabling employees to discover what their career anchors really are and which transitions would enable them to be met.

- They need to help employees discover what their potential is to undertake various transitions.

- They should be indicating what support by way of development and training they will be offering.

- They need to ensure that all of this information, the wants and needs of both parties, is communicated from one to the other successfully.

Ways of communicating the information necessary if career deals are to be successfully made will be reviewed more thoroughly in Chapter 8.

HR processes and the contracting process

Some HR processes which meet the needs of the contracting process already exist. Others need to be developed. The reason they are not already in existence is because the fundamental features of new employment relationships are only now becoming recognized:

- Learning today is not primarily about how to do jobs but rather about how to make transitions.

- Employee trust, motivation, and morale is so low that the unilateral imposition of an employment deal is ill advised.

- Transitions are so frequent that continuous negotiation and renegotiation of the employment relationship is essential.

Many of the HR processes now in use were designed for different times: job analysis, job evaluation, fast-track cohorts etc. They are now often inappropriate because each of them fails to take account of one or more of these three features. So in some cases we will be able to use what is available, in others we will have to invent. But in all our discussion of HR systems and processes, we have to remember that it is the principles and values implicit in contracting that are fundamental. If these are not subscribed to and acted upon, then no amount of systems will be of any use. Rather, they will simply serve to increase cynicism.

So the clear conclusions from this chapter are that:

- The organization's need for transitional flexibility can only be met if the individual needs of employees are also met by those same transitions.

- This can only occur through a contracting process between the parties.

- For contracting to work successfully, old HR processes and systems need to be adapted and new ones developed.

This chapter has covered the process of career contracting: how organizations and individuals can come to an agreement about which individuals should make which transitions. The next chapter looks at how organizations can provide the support for individuals to learn to become better at making transitions.

Some questions to think about

1. List the last three career transitions you have made. From your own perspective, what were the good and bad outcomes from each of them? In what ways if any have you changed as a person as a consequence of these transitions? How do you feel about these personal changes?

2. Administer Schein's Career Anchor Questionnaire to yourself. Alternatively, and much less validly, ask yourself which of his eight anchors is the one which in the final reckoning you could not do without. To what extent were your last three transitions consistent with this anchor? If they have been inconsistent, is this because personal or organizational circumstances forced you into a transition?

3. The fundamental features of career contracting are its two-way nature, its iterative character, its explicitness and its individualized quality. Which of these features does your organization find most difficult or is unwilling to accept? Using Figure 6.1 as a diagnostic, decide which stages of the process your organization is good at. Which is it bad at? Considering the latter, how would you address these shortcomings? What HR systems are in place which facilitate the process of career contracting? How appropriate are they, and do you need new ones? If so, which?

REFERENCES

1 Beatson, M. (1995) *Labour Market Flexibility*. Department of Employment Research Series 48. London: HMSO.

2 Rifkin, J. (1995) *The End of Work*. New York: Putnam.

3 McGill, M.E., Slocum, J.W. and Lei, D. (1992) 'Management practices in learning organisations'. *Organisational Dynamics* 22 (1): 5–18.

4 Nicholson, N. and West, M.A. (1988) *Managerial Job Change: Men and Women in Transition*. Cambridge: Cambridge University Press.

5 Herriot, P., Pemberton, C. and Hawtin, E. (1996) 'The career attitudes and intentions of managers in the finance sector'. *British Journal of Management* 7: 181–90.

6 Warr, P.B. (1993) 'Age and employment' in M. Dunnette, L. Hough and H. Triandis (eds) *Handbook of Industrial and Organizational Psychology*, vol. 4. Palo Alto: Consulting Psychologists Press.

7 Hutton, W. (1995) *The State We're In*. London: Jonathan Cape.

8 Driver, M.J. (1982) 'Career concepts: a new approach to career research', in R. Katz (ed.) *Career Issues in Human Resource Management*: Englewood Cliffs, NJ: Prentice-Hall.

9 Meyer, J.P. and Allen, N.J. (1984) 'Testing the side-bet theory of organisational commitment: Some methodological considerations'. *Journal of Applied Psychology* 69: 372–8.

10 Schein, E.H. (1993) *Career Anchors: Discovering your Real Values*, revised edn. London: Pfeiffer.

11 Herriot, P., Manning, W.E.G. and Kidd, J.M. (1997) 'The content of the psychological contract'. *British Journal of Management* 8: 151–62.

12 Brockner, A., Grover, S., Reed, T.G. and De Witte, R.L. (1992) 'Lay-offs, job insecurity, and survivors' work effort: evidence of an inverted U relationship'. *Academy of Management Journal* 35: 413–25.

13 DeMeuse, K.P., Vanderheiden, P.A. and Bergmann, T.J. (1994) 'Announced layoffs: their effect on corporate financial performance'. *Human Resource Management* 33 (4): 509–30.

14 Cascio, W.F. (1994) 'Downsizing: what do we know? What have we learned?' *Academy of Management Executive* 7: 95–104.

15 Latack, J.C. (1990) 'Organizational restructuring and career management: from outplacement and survival to inplacement', in G. Ferris and K. Rowland (eds) *Research in Personnel and Human Resources Management*, vol. 8. Greenwich, CT: JAI Press.

16 Herriot, P. and Pemberton, C. (1997) 'Facilitating new deals'. *Human Resource Management Journal* 7 (1): 45–56.

17 Herriot, P. and Pemberton, C. (1996) 'Contracting careers'. *Human Relations* 49 (6): 757–90.

18 Hirsh, W., and Jackson, C. (1996) 'Strategies for career development: promise, practice, and pretence'. Brighton: Institute for Employment Studies, Report 305.

Development for transition

7

HITTING THE GROUND RUNNING: THE ORGANIZATIONAL PERSPECTIVE

If careers are a sequence of transitions, then career development is by definition development for transition. As individuals prepare for, encounter and adjust to each transition, they learn not only the new knowledge and skills associated with the specific new role to which they are moving. They may also learn how better to make transitions in general; how better to prepare for, encounter and adjust to new roles so that they can get up to full speed faster next time round. From the organizational perspective, then, career development is a matter of learning to learn quicker and better. The business benefits are clear: an internal labour market full of flexible learners offering seamless transitions when the business needs them.

Yet relatively few employers have got round to thinking this way about development. For most, the idea is associated with preparation for one sort of transition only: upward movement to positions further up the hierarchy. And even within that limited definition, attention has been focused on development for top management. The top 200 and their degree of readiness to move onto the board have recently obsessed both boards themselves and also corporate HR. It is those companies which have realized that they depend upon the transition learning of everyone, and especially the workforce, which are the exceptions. Automobile manufacturers, for example, such as Ford, Vauxhall,[1] and Rover, have pioneered development for all.

A further obstacle to the achievement of learning how to make transitions lies in the assumptions held by many about how people best learn. It is rightly normally assumed that learning is achieved through experience. But while experience is usually a necessary condition for learning, it is not a sufficient one. Granted there are several preferred styles of learning,[2] all authorities are convinced that experience alone does not reliably deliver transition learning. An employee can have a series of varied jobs, each of which requires new skills and knowledge. Yet they may be no quicker at acquiring skills and knowledge when they move to job ten than they were when they moved to job two. It is only when we recognize the need for two intellectual activities as well as the need for experience that transition learning can occur.[3]

'Guidelines' at Vauxhall Motors

- Vauxhall's development philosophy derives from its total quality management policy. Vauxhall believes that this implies improvement not only in jobs but also in people. Investing in their development is therefore a legitimate business objective.

- The key focus of the programme and the first major event is the guidance interview. This enables strengths and weaknesses to be assessed, and development opportunities identified in the context of a restructured organization.

- Action plans are derived, and signed by both the employee and the guidance counsellor as an indication of commitment. Whether or not these are shared with the individual's line manager is entirely up to them.

- Bespoke learning packages and equipment are available, with external training providers attending the plant to fit in with shift patterns.

- Learning opportunities provided on site are all related, directly or indirectly, to work. However, counsellors help employees find outside opportunities for non-vocational topics.

- The Guidelines scheme has been in existence for 2½ years. It has been used by 60 percent of the workforce, including managers, and provides 5,000 learning hours per month.

- Drop-out from the programme is minimal, and organizational commitment has increased.

Two necessary intellectual activities

The first of these is **reflection**. We need to reflect upon our actions and experiences in order to gain meaning from them. We need to be able to describe for ourselves and others what it was we did, how we did it, what was its context, and what were its outcomes. We also need to make sense of these data. Why did we do it at all? Why did we do it like we did? Why did it turn out like it did?

The second intellectual activity is revising our frames of reference, our ways of thinking about something. Chris Argyris[4] calls this **double-loop learning**. It depends upon experience and reflection having both occurred. We are forced to revise our frames of reference when the data from our experience and the only explanations we can find for them fit into none of our existing frameworks. In other words, we are forced to change our frameworks to accommodate the evidence. And with new frameworks, we can conceive of the possibility of doing different things, or of doing things differently, next time round.

There are all sorts of barriers to these two intellectual activities occurring:

- The Anglo-Saxon business culture is action oriented and short term;[5] intellectual activities have no obvious immediate pay-off.

- It is individualist in its orientation,[6] and hence assumes that learning is an individual rather than a social activity.

- We are apt to assimilate the evidence to our frameworks rather than accommodate our frameworks to the evidence.[7] We grow fond of our frameworks, which fit us like a comfortable old pullover.

- We learn most from unexpected outcomes, and given our eternal optimism, these are often our mistakes and failures.

- But we usually conceal or rationalize mistakes and failures in order to conserve our reputation and our self-esteem, and to avoid punishment.

- We do not know how best to engage in such intellectual activities together in the organizational context.

In terms of transition learning, these general considerations about the nature of learning imply the need to reflect on each transition. What was done by way of preparation, we need to ask. What happened when we first encountered the new reality? What adjustments were made by us and by others? How quickly did we become fully functional in our new role? Why did things happen this way? And why were the outcomes so good (moderate, bad)?

The intellectual framework

If transition learning is to occur, though, we also need to be prepared to change our intellectual framework. We may need to adapt the way we think about transitions. As we will argue, organizations may need to stop viewing transitions from their own perspective only, and start considering individuals' perspectives too. This will require them to stop intellectualizing the episode as if the only consideration were how quickly skill learning and adaptation occur. They will have to start to realize the profound personal and emotional factors that affect individuals in transition.

But the impetus for such reframing will only come from reflecting upon the evidence. We may ask ourselves such questions as:

- Why, despite top-class prior training and a well-proven induction process, does performance take such a long time to peak?
- Why do so many leave within the first two months?
- Why are some teams so much better than others at assimilating new members?

The answers we come up with to these questions may relate to lack of confidence, resentment at having been forced to make a transition, incompatibility of the new role with home responsibilities, loss of workmates, loss of dignity and status, lack of support, and so on. Transitions are not simply learning opportunities, we may conclude: they are also life events. And this conclusion may lead us to manage transitions in new ways.

HITTING THE GROUND LIMPING: THE INDIVIDUALS' PERSPECTIVE

So what is individuals' perspective on development? How do they perceive the various possible ways of preparing to make career transitions? The answer, as usual, is that it all depends. The danger lies in fitting the wide variety of career transitions that people experience into a single explanatory framework. Perceptions of our own career transitions are likely to vary according to:

- The **nature** of the transition: is it a role enlargement or a role change; a cross-functional move; a move out of a full-time contract; from one form of career to another?
  - a role change may be seen as a slightly anxiety provoking but highly exciting opportunity
  - a cross-functional move could be a huge risk, an irrevocable step, and a loss of professional identity; or it could be an opportunity to break free from an occupational straitjacket
  - leaving a full-time contract might be a leap to freedom, or into the abyss.

- Its **predictability**: has it been signalled in advance? Do we know when it is going to happen? There is a distinction between just-in-time and only just in time.
  - uncertainty generates helplessness and anxiety
  - advance notice permits us to get ourselves used to the idea and prepare ourselves for the change.

- Its **optionality**: have we had any say in the occurrence and nature of the transition? Has it been the subject of career contracting?
  - imposition may generate resentment and hostility, or helplessness
  - choice can result in commitment to the transition and motivation to succeed.

- Its **clarity**: has the post-transition role been clearly described?
  - if it is too prescribed, we may feel constricted
  - if it is unspecified, anxious and impotent.

- Its **justification**: have the reasons for the transition been explained?
  - if the attribution is to the external business environment, fine but fatalistic
  - if it is internal to ourselves, our self-esteem may be threatened.

- Its **implications**: what is it likely to mean for us subsequently?
  - more free time, less money – survival concerns loom large
  - more work, less free time – lifestyle and health may be a worry
  - big bucks now, but will we have a job in three years' time?

Resilience

How we respond, then, will depend on how much we have learned about how to make transitions. It will also depend on the sort of individual we are. As we have shown, the identity of our main career anchor will have a profound effect. But so, according to recent rhetoric, will a more general personal characteristic: our resilience.[8] If we have to withstand uncertainty and anxiety, threats to our identity and our lifestyle, then we have to be survivors or we are sunk. As Slocum discovered:

> There was not a moment to spare, and I saw clearly that if I failed now all might be lost. I sprang from the oars to my feet, and lifting the anchor above my head, threw it clear just as she was turning over. I grasped her gunwale and held on as she turned bottom up, for I suddenly remembered that I could not swim . . . Three times I had been under water in trying to right the dory, and I was just saying 'Now I lay me', when I was seized by a determination to try yet once more, so that no one of the prophets of evil I had left behind me could say, 'I told you so'. Whatever the danger may have been, much or little, I can truly say that the moment was the most serene of my life.

Career resilience has been so described as to appear an individual characteristic that is developed in an individual way.

> Individuals who are career resilient contribute skills aligned with business needs, are dedicated to continuous learning and committed to personal excellence, have an attitude that is focused but flexible, and deliver solid performance in support of organisational goals for as long as they are part of the organisation. [They] stand ready to reinvent themselves to keep pace with change [and] take responsibility for their own career management. [They have] the ability to adapt to changing circumstances, even when the circumstances are discouraging or disruptive.[9]

In order to develop such resilience, people have to become more **self-reliant**, we are told. Self-reliance is:

> The ability to actively manage one's work life in a rapidly changing environment; the attitude of being self-employed, whether inside or outside an organisation.

It requires self-confidence, a high need for achievement, and the willingness to take risks. In sum, it needs a combination of the Archangel Gabriel and Superperson.

Unless we are careful, we are back into the harsh climate of social Darwinism here. It is all down to the individual, Me plc. Organizations as a whole can merely provide the environment within which the species adapts or dies out, we are told. Line management is generally proving a broken reed when it comes to career help, and indeed often knows as little as their subordinates about the career context. The HR function has been stripped down, and anyway it is far too busy firefighting on top management's behalf to help the employees. HR professionals are business people now, not do-gooders. People can rely on no-one else for help: it is everyone for himself in the competitive bearpit. It is all up to them as individuals. They are either survivors or not. Develop yourself or perish, or so runs the story.

Yet to leave it all to the mechanism of the survival of the fittest is a counsel of despair. The organization can so manage transitions as to enable employees to learn from the experience of transition. More important, it can facilitate the more profound developmental tasks facing people who make the bigger transitions. When identity or survival are at risk, we need help. We may have to make major personal adjustments that require us radically to redefine our identity and values. The recommendations which follow are based on the fundamental belief that identities were originally formed, and subsequently change and develop, as a result of social activity. We need a little help from our friends if we are to learn from our transitions.

LEARNING FROM ROLE TRANSITION

The key to facilitating career development, then, is the management of transitions. The first task of transition management is to help individuals make a particular transition as effectively as possible. The second is to enable them to learn from the process of that transition how to make the next one more effectively still, whatever it may require. The more skilled people become at making transitions, the bigger and the quicker the tran-

British Airways

One organization which has recognized that many transitions are profound personal events and require organizational support is British Airways (BA). In late 1996 it reconfigured a predominantly outplacement provision and called it Career Link. Its purpose is to help those who might be vulnerable to change, and it is open to all. Through workshops, Career Link aids networking, assertiveness, interview skills and the consideration of alternative careers. The result is to stimulate career thinking, enable staff to take more responsibility for themselves, and raise the possibility of flexible contracting and other internal or external options.

Career Link feeds into two other provisions: Skills Link and Quest. The former is brokered by a training manager who will call up behavioural or technical training on the Career Link graduate's behalf. The latter is a management development centre which is essentially a self-directed learning centre, using videos, CD-ROMS, etc. Staff can refer themselves to Quest; they do not have to be graduates of Career Link.

Cable and Wireless

Cable and Wireless (C&W) expressly states that it is trying to help individuals become more career resilient with its Career Action Centre. The aim is to 'increase your value to the organization while sharpening your own most valuable skills and competencies'. This provision is to enable employees to take action; it is enabling rather than doing. An initial assessment of current skills against future needs is made by the individual employee. The purpose of this assessment is not to find a new job internally or externally, but rather to help individuals achieve more of their potential within the organization. The product is an action plan for development, and attendees are referred by their line manager or they self-refer.

sitions they will be capable of making. Hence, career development involves learning how to make bigger transitions better.

How might role transitions be effectively managed so as to optimize the learning of the preparation, encounter and adjustment skills of transition between roles? If people are going to learn, they must first experience transitions in all their phases. Predictability is a crucial feature of a role transition. The amount of notice of the transition that individuals are given is of paramount importance, for several reasons:

- They need time to tie up the ends of their present role.

- They benefit from 'anticipatory socialization': imagining what the new role is like and practising it 'in the head'.

- They can use the opportunity to contact the present role incumbent.

- They may also make contact with their new boss and colleagues.

Also important is clarity. How much can people find out in advance about this particular job? How easy is it for them to discover what are its main tasks, and how frequent, important, and difficult is each of them? Who are the main customers or clients, internal or external, for their work? Who will they be working with and who will they be working for? Preparation is, after all, a time of expectation.

Forms of preparation for transition

Again, given this information, several forms of **preparation** become possible. People may play through their future posting in their minds if they have an idea of what they are going to be doing;[10] or they may take active steps rapidly to acquire skills or knowledge which they feel they are short of but will need for the new role. There are several ways in which this can be managed. One of the most useful is for the individual to be given time to go and see the job being done in person, and meet and ask questions of the present job incumbent or a colleague. Another is for some of the tools or products of the trade to be made available in advance of joining, for example, some technical drawings for an engineer, some product descriptions for a salesperson, recent technical publications for a research chemist, and so on.

The **encounter** phase is also assisted by such simple and obvious measures. To know what to expect and to have already met some of one's new colleagues is a major boost to the confidence of the newcomer, since encounter is all about emotions and perceptions. Yet all this can be undone by the most ludicrous oversights. The basic necessities, be it tools, telephone, computer, uniform and a person to receive them may not have been ready for the newcomer on arrival. The stories of bright-eyed bushy-tailed young people arriving for their first real job and finding themselves totally unexpected are legion. They are also tragic. By way of contrast, one of the authors of this book was presented with a bunch of flowers on his first day at work in the Netherlands.

It is the adjustment phase, however, that is probably the most important in role or in any other work transition. In terms of the actual work of the new job, individuals have to decide to what extent they retain their own methods and practices and to what extent they adapt their ways of working entirely to the norms of their new colleagues.[11] Either way it is a time of change: change in the person and change in the role. Total conformity may inhibit organizational innovation, since new people can import new ideas about how to do things better. The management of newcomers is therefore crucial; when their manager seeks to learn from them and is seen to do so, then two-way adaptation can occur. People get up to speed more quickly when they have been able to import as much as possible of their previous knowledge and skills into the new job.

However, the biggest single method of getting up to speed is by assisted practice on the job. Sitting next to Nellie has long been ridiculed, but planned and structured on-the-job training and coaching is often the most effective method of all.[12] Nellie may be a manager, supervisor, or trainer, but she is just as likely to be a colleague. The fundamentals of training are also the fundamentals of sitting next to Nellie:

- Discover which job skills need to be acquired.

- Have clear plans, structure, targets, and objectives.

- Assess and feed back progress.

- Select and train suitable Nellies.

Examples from either end of the organizational spectrum demonstrate the value of on-the-job training. In both cases it is crucial that the newcomer get up to speed quickly.

At the other end of the hierarchy, in a large finance sector organization, the chairman coaches all new members of the board, both in the general rules of the board game and in particular in how to deal with non-executive directors. If new board members have not reached full speed within one year (and meetings are only bi-monthly), then they are considered failures.

Vickers

In Vickers, a diverse manufacturing company, new appointees to senior positions are assigned a mentor from among the executive cadre, and are sent on specially designed training courses.

McDonald's

McDonald's, with its very temporary workforce, allocates a 'buddy' to new 'crew members'. This buddy has been trained to help the newcomers work through their training manual, and the degree of learning achieved is assessed by unobtrusive observation by a manager.

Organizational socialization

Adjustment, though, covers so much more than the work itself. Recent research on organizational socialization[13] and organizational fit[14] suggests that new entrants to a role may have to:

- adapt their behaviour so as to be accepted by their new workmates

- understand the history and the politics of their new workgroup

- master a new vocabulary, or new uses for old terms

- accept (or conform to) a different set of goals and value priorities.

These adjustments are likely to be greater when the transition is from another organization. But there are differences in subcultures within organizations which suggest that they will be needed for many internal transitions too.[15] The allocation of an existing member of staff to help the newcomer on his or her first day may only serve in the first instance to enable them to find their feet and discover the geography. But if the person allocated is from the newcomer's workgroup, then there is always the possibility of the relationship developing into a mentoring one. A local mentor is very helpful in pointing out behavioural norms, goals, and values, and in giving the historical and political information that only an insider can know.

In order to learn from transitions, we need to be able to focus back and reflect upon the way we negotiated the various stages. The really important developmental task is to learn from the transition once it has happened. Instead of saying 'Now that you've settled in, let's talk about your role', line managers need to say to newcomers: 'Let's look back at your transition and see what we can learn from it.' And if organizations are to learn as well as individuals, they will be asking 'How well did we as a group manage Chris's entry? How can we better manage entry in general?' All this is a far cry from leaving career-resilient employees to sink or swim in the organizational pond. Learning from transitions requires management intervention and colleague collaboration to ensure the transition phases are negotiated well. It needs conscious directed reflection on the transition process. Finally, it requires challenge to our views of ourselves and our capabilities.

The traditional view of transition would include stabilization at this point. What is more, it would suggest that all the three previous stages were leading up to this final and lengthy period, when both organization and individual can at last concentrate upon performance. The fact that this scenario now sounds so passé only emphasizes the pressure upon the individual to get up to speed as fast as possible. And the danger of this pressure is that employees are rushed into decisions and ways of working which are suboptimal. The importance of the organization's management of the first three stages is therefore enhanced. For only if they are well managed will individuals learn from the experience.

TRANSITIONS AND THE SELF

One of the fundamental mistakes that organizations continue to make is to ignore the affective side of transitions. Indeed, they even failed for some time to understand the depth of feeling caused by compulsory redundancies, both in those who were made redundant and in those who remained.[16] There are some transitions (for example, out of the organization unwillingly, or from full-time to part-time work, or demotions signalling a change in career trajectory) which cause such strong feelings that even those employees who are spectators feel strong anxiety for themselves and maybe guilt about the sufferers.[17] On the other side of the emotional coin, many organizations repeatedly neglect the potentially motivating positive emotional effects of role changes,[18] be they upwards or sideways.

In order to support effectively people learning from transitions, however, it is not enough to recognize that strong feelings may be involved. We need to understand why they arise, so that we know what to do to help. Our explanation is in terms of our view of ourselves, our self-conceptions. These can be categorized as follows:[19]

- Our **self-esteem**: do we have a reasonably good feeling about our own abilities and actions?

- Our **identity**: do we have a coherent notion of who we are, and is that notion stable over time?

- Our **agency**: do we feel that we can control outcomes that are important to us? Are we capable of making choices?

Self-esteem

Self-esteem is related to our confidence in our abilities and our perception of being valued for what we do and who we are. Clearly several transitions are in danger of damaging our self-esteem, others are likely to enhance it. In particular, moves out of full-time work, out of the organization, or down the hierarchy may well be damaging. Promotions, role changes, and allocation to more prestigious projects will probably enhance self-esteem.

Identity

We have already discussed identity and transition (see p. 92). Clearly, the loss of one's job and consequent exit from the organization is likely to threaten such elements of identity as breadwinner and organizational member. But other transitions, such as a move out of one's function, may also threaten identity, in this case, professional identity. The coherence of one's identity may suffer if, for example, the transition creates a disjuncture between organizational and parental elements of identity: I may get promoted and identify more with the organization and its top management, but work such long hours that I never see my children during the week. And our stability is threatened when transitions come thick and fast, stretching our capacity to incorporate new roles into our changing notions of who we are. Sometimes a single transition can incorporate a promotion, a change of function, and a change of organization.

Agency

Finally, how much do we feel in control of transitions? In cases where we have initiated the move, or where we have been given a real choice whether or not to make it, we still have control. But so many transitions are imposed by the organization, often claiming that it had no choice in the prevailing business climate. Our sense of being agents rather than victims is a fundamental aspect of the self. Its opposite, learned helplessness, is personally and organizationally crippling. This is why the idea of career contracting, that is, having a two-way dialogue, is fundamental to establishing a sense of agency.

The frequency of the following moves has been steadily increasing:

- involuntary moves out of organizations

- moves away from a full-time contract

- cross-functional moves

- changes in career type and trajectory.

Thus attention needs to be paid to the threats to the self-concept experienced by those in such transitions, and also by those who believe that they are likely to suffer them. Such attention is warranted both from the perspective of individual well-being, and also from that of organizational effectiveness. Employees with low self-esteem are unlikely to attempt new learning. Those whose identity is threatened are going to be alienated from both work and organization. And those who feel helpless and manipulated are likely to keep their heads down, take no risks, and wait for a good opportunity to leave.

Even the potentially self-enhancing transitions may also threaten the self if managed wrongly. Damage to self-esteem can so easily follow, for example, from a promotion from one of the remaining levels of the hierarchy to another. This latter level may be different qualitatively in the knowledge and skills involved. If individuals receive little support in such major transitions, their self-esteem can take a fearful battering, and their 'failure' may become a lasting black mark against their name. Any notion of development is out of the question; rather, regression and damage to the self are the outcomes. Contrast the self-reports of the biggest learning leaps of their careers from those whose new boss allowed them to undertake projects far more stretching than any they had done before. The difference was, they had the promise that the boss would carry the can if they came unstuck.[20]

MANAGING TRANSITIONAL AFFECT

It is not sufficient to talk of the need for career resilience to overcome these threats to the self. Some have a high level of such resilience, others do not and will never acquire it. As with learning, so with affective issues: it is the responsibility of management to provide the context and the occasion for such fundamental and personal issues to be addressed while transitions are occurring. If they fail to do so, they will be responsible both for personal suffering and also for a loss of organizational effectiveness. How are senior managers to respond to such a challenge when most of them seldom pay attention to the affective features of the organization's life, or even, perhaps, of their own?

The role of others

As with transition learning, so with the affective consequences of actual or anticipated transition. It is the task of those who manage transitions to set up opportunities for social relationships. For our self-conceptions are socially derived. It is others who can help us to re-establish our self-esteem. It is others who can enable us to adapt our identities to the new realities while maintaining a degree of coherence and stability. It is others who can demonstrate that by acting together we can affect outcomes ourselves.

What forms of social process are needed to achieve these supportive ends? Part of the answer lies in self-help groups consisting of those who are already adapted to the transition in question and those who are approaching and encountering it, or are just initially adapting. The model is almost that of Alcoholics Anonymous: 'My name is Mary and I'm a part-timer!' Such support can enhance self-esteem, since people feel valued because other group members are concerned for them. They establish a firmer identity because they can see that others are secure in their new role and can see some benefits. And they get a sense of greater agency because they soon learn from others the best ways to make the new role suit their own needs. For a middle manager to encourage the formation of such groups requires a sense of security not always apparent in a role now as much at risk as any other.

KEY POINT

One often ignored identity issue is that facing women entering management for the first time. The stereotype of management is traditionally extremely masculine, and women frequently ask themselves whether their identities as women will be threatened or compromised. A number of women's networks now offers support to women in this major transition, given that there may not be any other women managers nearby to share experiences with. These networks also offer help and information to women going on maternity leave and then subsequently managing their re-entry to work with its attendant issues of working hours and child care.

Actions of support in the transition process

However, there are other actions that senior managers can take directly to support those personally affected in transition. One, which runs counter to the current tendency to discriminate between core and other employees, is to make explicit attempts to demonstrate how much they value particular groups for what they offer.

Consider the insurance industry. It is now the youngest and lowest grade employees who get business and deal with customers at all hours over the phone. Many are part -time, most work shifts. Yet all the traditional signals of being valued indicate to these vital workers that they are the least valued of all: status, basic pay, degree of autonomy and trust, contact with senior managers etc. An entirely new approach to valuing such staff would be to take seriously the idea of psychological contracting (pp. 21–2). This would mean asking each individual what working arrangements would suit them so as best to fit in both with their personal lives and also with the organization's need for labour at particular times. Both First Direct and Lloyds TSB have given teams of telesales staff and their supervisors autonomy in allocating work to suit lifestyle needs.

As with transition learning, so with handling the far more important affective side of transitions: a particular transition can have very different consequences:

• It may lead to catastrophic personal and organizational consequences.

• It may be painful and temporarily disabling at a time when energies need to be directed at making the transition.

- It may result in temporary anxiety, soon to be replaced by new-found confidence.[21]

- It may be hugely affirming and self-enhancing.

KEY POINT

An ever more frequent transition now is from working for a company to working for a merged company of which this is now a part. Such transitions can go either way, for good or ill. After a recent merger in the pharmaceutical industry, many new teams were formed out of the old ones. They needed to find ways of coming to terms with the merger and with each other. The merged company ran three-day sessions for each new team to get to know each other and to discuss how they were going to work together. It was a way of dealing with negative feelings in a positive way and giving teams a good start after a painful transition.

How any one transition is managed will partly determine what sort of outcome occurs. The evidence is overwhelming that the way in which redundancies, for example, are handled is just as important in determining employees' reactions as the redundancy terms themselves.[22] But the key issue is not what happens affectively in any single transition. It is how we can learn to better manage the affective side of transitions in general.

Again, as with transition learning, the answer is experience, reflection, and changing our personal frameworks as a consequence. However, to reflect on how we felt in the course of a transition is far harder than reflecting on what we did. And changing our framework for how we construe ourselves and our feelings is hardest of all. One of the hardest tasks of those who seek to counsel people suffering stress at work is to help them reframe the way they think of themselves. Some have only succeeded in adapting to constant change by splitting themselves between their private and their work identities. The values which underpin these two parts of the self may be completely incompatible, and the consequences for personal and organizational health and well-being may sometimes be devastating.

The only way to help individuals address such profound elements of development is through skilled facilitation on a one-to-one or group basis. However, there is no reason whatever why self-supporting groups and networks may not learn from counsellors how to manage this sort or personal learning and development for themselves. How to support each other is one of the most vital skills to learn in a climate of endless change and constant transitions. It is also one of the least valued and the least developed. The one exception to this generalization is redundancy (outplacement) counselling. It is generally recognized here that skilled counsellors can sometimes help redundant employees to reframe their self-conceptions. The outcome is sometimes to turn that transition into a chance to upgrade a valued part of the self which they had kept hidden from themselves and others.

WHITHER DEVELOPMENT?

This chapter has offered a radical view of development. Most definitions currently in favour are derived from the organization's perspective. More specifically, such definitions ask: what competencies will individuals have to develop in order to meet the future skill requirements of the organization? What technical knowledge will they need? What will they need to pick up about how the organization works, its processes and culture? A concession to individual preferences and capabilities is made by offering somewhat different alternative sets of required competencies, for example, general managerial, supervisory, or expert technical ones.

There is also currently fashionable a less specific view of development, which suggests that change is essentially unpredictable. Hence the balance and nature of the skills and knowledge required is unspecifiable in detail, and the most that can be said is that employees will have to be good at continuous learning. They will also have to be resilient to cope with constant transition.

Clearly, the more specific of these two views of development is likely to lead to development plans for individuals which the organization can help the individual realize. The less specific view leads to a more individualistic approach, according to which adaptability and resilience are needed by anyone who is to survive, and people simply have to develop these characteristics for themselves.

Our own view of development is more specific than this latter perspective, since it focuses upon learning and the affective inputs and outcomes of transitions. Granted our assumption that transitions and not jobs are the fundamental element of careers, then development has to be for transitions. And granted our second assumption, that careers have to be contracted not imposed, then the individual's perspective as well as the organization's has to be considered. While organizations have only recently come to realize the impact of affective responses on organizational performance and morale, individuals have always been affected more emotionally than intellectually by transitions. Our review of development has therefore concentrated as much upon the development of the self as upon the acquisition of knowledge and skills.

But this does not imply that our analysis has ignored business needs. On the contrary, we have emphasized that individual transitions are necessary to **support** the recurrent changes in business direction. Depending on whether the organization is growing or contracting, looking short or longer term, or centralizing or devolving, different sorts of individual transitions will be necessary. In this chapter we have looked at the sort of organizational support and development required to make transitions successfully. In the next, we will consider the information that people need to help them to choose and to make transitions. And not least among that information are some messages about the sorts of learning they will need to engage in.

Some questions to think about

1. How long did it take you to get up to speed in your last job transition? What hindered and what helped? What did you learn from making the transition, and how did you learn it?

2. When you were adjusting to your last transition, what was the balance between your adapting yourself to the role and your adjusting the role to yourself? Was this the balance you would have preferred? Did you pay more attention to the tasks of the new role and the skills you would need, or to being accepted, fitting in, and understanding the politics and culture? In retrospect, did you focus on the right things?

3. Does your organization recognize the threats posed to employees' well-being and identity by certain transitions? What does it do about them? What could it do?

REFERENCES

1   Parsons, G. and Stickland, E. (1996) 'How Vauxhall Motors is getting its employees on the road to lifelong learning'. *European Journal of Work and Organisational Psychology* 5 (4): 597–608.
2   Mumford, A. (1993) *Management Development: Strategies for Action*, 2nd edn. London: IPM Press.

3   Kolb, D. (1984) *Experiential Learning*. Englewood Cliffs, NJ: Prentice-Hall.
4   Argyris, C. (1993) *Knowledge for Action*. New York: Jossey Bass.
5   Trompenaars, F. (1993) *Riding the Waves of Culture*. London: Nicholas Brealey.
6   Hofstede, G. (1980) *Culture's Consequences*. London: Sage.
7   Isenberg, D.J. (1986) 'Thinking and managing: a verbal protocol analysis of managerial problem solving'. *Academy of Management Journal* 29 (4): 775–88.
8   Waterman, R.H., Waterman, J.A. and Collard, B.A. (1994) 'Toward a career resilient workforce'. *Harvard Business Review* 72 (4): 87–95.
9   Collard, B.A., Epperheimer, J.W. and Saign, D. (1996) *Career Resilience in a Changing Workplace*. Columbus, OH: ERIC Clearinghouse, Ohio State University.
10   Wanous, J.P., Poland, T.D., Premack, S.L. and Davis, K.S. (1992) 'The effects of met expectations on newcomer attitudes and behaviours: a review and meta-analysis'. *Journal of Applied Psychology* 77 (2): 288–97.
11   Stephens, G.K. (1994) 'Crossing internal career boundaries: the state of research on subjective career transitions'. *Journal of Management* 20 (4): 479–501.
12   Cannell, M. (1997) 'Practice makes perfect'. *People Management* 97 (3): 27–33.
13   Chao, G.T., O'Leary-Kelly, A.M., Wolf, S., Klein, H.J. and Gardner, P.D. (1994) 'Organisational socialisation: its content and consequences'. *Journal of Applied Psychology* 79 (7): 730–43.
14   Schneider, B., Kristof-Brown, A.L., Goldstein, H.W. and Brent Smith, D. (1997) 'What is this thing called fit?' in N. Anderson and P. Herriot (eds) *International Handbook of Assessment and Selection*. Chichester: Wiley.
15   Van Maanen, J. and Barley, S.R. (1984) 'Occupational communities: culture and control in organizations', in B.M. Staw and L.L.Cummings (eds) *Research in Organizational Behaviour*, vol. 6. Greenwich, CT: JAI Press.
16   Noer, D.M. (1993) *Healing the Wounds*. San Francisco: Jossey Bass.
17   Konovsky, M.A. and Brockner, J. (1993) 'Managing victim and survivor lay-off reactions: a procedural justice perspective', in R. Cropanzano (ed.) *Justice in the Workplace*. Hillsdale, NJ: Lawrence Erlbaum.
18   Herriot, P., Pemberton, C. and Hawtin, E. (1996) 'The career attitudes and intentions of managers in the finance sector'. *British Journal of Management* 7: 181–90.
19   Steele, C.M. (1988) 'The psychology of self affirmation: sustaining the integrity of the self', in L. Berkowitz (ed.) *Advances in Experimental Social Psychology*. San Diego, CA: Academic Press.
20   Kotter, J.P. (1982) *The General Managers*. New York: Free Press.
21   Nicholson, M. and West, M.A. (1988) *Managerial Job Change: Men and Women in Transition*. Cambridge: Cambridge University Press.
22   Brockner, J., Konorsky, M., Cooper-Schneider, R., Folger, R., Martin, C. and Bies, R.J. (1994) 'Interactive effects of procedural justice and outcome negativity on victims and survivors of job loss'. *Academy of Management Journal* 37 (2): 397–409.

Information exchange: dialogue and transitions 8

Information and career contracting

The sun, the wind, the sea and his chronometer gave Joshua Slocum all the information he needed. All he had to do was gather that information and make sense of it:

> The Southern Cross I saw every night abeam. The sun every morning came up astern; every evening it went down ahead. I wished for no other compass to guide me, for these were true. If I doubted my reckoning after a long time at sea, I verified it by reading the clock aloft made by the Great Architect, and it was right.

It was not quite that simple. Slocum knew what to look for and how to interpret it as the result of a lifetime's experience as a sailor. But the information was there for him when he needed it. The same cannot be said about career transitions. We do not know for sure what these are going to be or when they will occur. And that is not the only information we need.

Once again, we need to return to our model of contracting the employment relationship, of doing deals (see Figure 6.1, p. 98). This model makes clear the crucial importance of information to the success of the entire contracting process. The career deal has to be based on the wants of the two parties, and what they are each prepared to offer the other. The purpose of the information exchange is to enable each party to make a realistic offer to the other on the basis of which a mutually acceptable deal is likely to be agreed. Figure 8.1 presents the information flows required.

This figure assumes that the two parties know what they want:

- Arrows 1 and 2 feed into the organization's decision as to what transitions it can offer.

- Arrows 3 and 4 feed into individuals' decisions as to what they can offer.

- It follows that only when organizations know what individuals want and vice versa can sensible offers be made by either party.

- The success of arrow 5, the negotiation stage, depends upon the offers being directed at the other party's needs, and therefore based on correct information about those needs.

ORGANIZATIONAL WANTS AND OFFERS

So how viable and practicable is this model of information exchange and dialogue? A fundamental question to start with is: are organizations capable of knowing what their own needs/wants are? Our argument so far has been that most of them have some ideas about the overall numbers and the balance of roles and employment contracts which they presently require. However, such estimates are likely to be shortlived, since they are apt at ever-decreasing intervals to swing from one phase to another: from expansion to contraction, long- to short-termism, and centralization to devolution (or the reverse directions). Thus their wants in terms of the transitions they would like employees to make are likely to change radically and repeatedly.

As we have seen, each of these phases leads to very different transition needs from its opposite:

- **Expansion** into new markets may be accomplished through organic growth, in which case there will be a lot of movement into new roles. Thorough organizations will try to establish the competencies needed to fulfil these roles. If the expansion is through acquisition, then the transitions may be mostly into bigger but similar roles. **Contraction**, however, is likely to lead to moves to part-time or temporary contracts, redundancies, and more work for those who are left.

- **Long-termism** implies moves across a sequence of positions for development purposes, **short-termism** a concentration on performance in the present job and a lack of transition opportunities; or, if transitions do occur, they are to where the organization has the greatest need. They are unlikely to be developmental.

- **Centralization** implies less local, more cross-business transitions determined on the basis of corporate need. **Devolution** puts local manage-

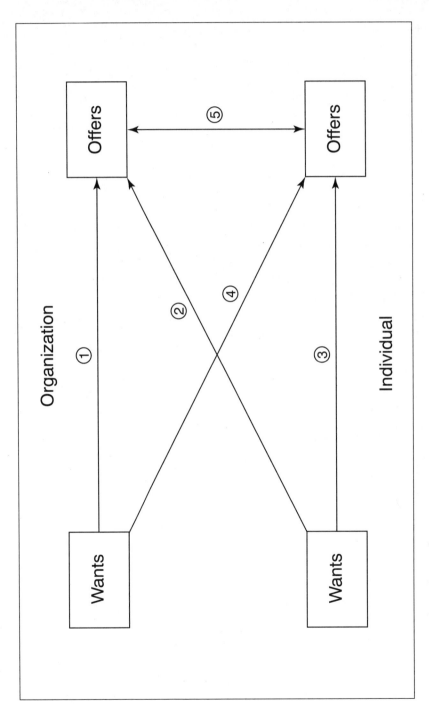

Figure 8.1   Information exchange

ment in charge of the dialogue, with the consequence that the range of transitions will be more limited, and information about corporate-wide opportunities less available.

While top managements may know which phases of the three dimensions of change they are in, they may well have little idea of how imminent the transition to the opposite phase actually is. So, for example, organizations with fine lists of detailed and specific competencies which they believe will be needed as they continue to expand may suddenly be faced with the same old requirements for redundancies as they are forced (or choose) to contract.

The question therefore is: what information can organizations give to employees about the nature of the transitions they want them to make now; and about those they are likely to want in the future? There are two very different answers to the two parts of this question. Organizations should be able to use resource planning methods to answer such questions as:

- How many temps are we going to need over Christmas?

- Are we recruiting enough graduate engineers, given the current turn-over rate?

- Given our recent delayering, what should now be the approximate span of control of first-line supervisors, and so how many more/fewer of them do we need?

- How many and which jobs are going to be lost as a consequence of our decision to centralize our cheque processing in two large units?

- In the presently ongoing merger, which roles do not need to be duplicated in the merged company?

- What implications does our decision to provide a 24-hour service have for flexible contracts?

- What are the competencies which are needed to perform different sorts of work at different levels at present?

- What levels of these competencies exist in the workforce, and where are the main shortfalls and excesses?

British Petroleum

High-potential young managers from various parts of British Petroleum (BP) were not experiencing the rapid promotion they had expected when they joined the company. This was due to the reduced numbers of promotions available in the tight business conditions of the early 1990s. Their response to this disappointment was very much affected by their understanding of the company's business situation. First, they were well aware of what was happening in other major UK employing organizations, and felt that their futures were at least as promising in BP as elsewhere. Second, they had good information on what was happening to BP's business, and how this was affecting jobs in different parts of the company. They also had fairly frequent opportunities to discuss their careers with people who had a broad view of the business. These factors combined to keep this group of young managers in the company, and by and large they felt well treated in a difficult situation.

Bias towards competencies

If the principles of career dealing are to be followed, then such information should be communicated to employees as soon as possible. But there is another sort of information which can only be communicated in a different way. The future transitional needs of the business are unlikely to be capable of the same level of specification as the current ones. Efforts at formal succession planning over three moves ahead have been given up long ago,[1] not least because the job for which the planning is carried out is likely to have changed or disappeared by the time the succession would have occurred. What benefit there is in succession planning comes from understanding who you have and what their capabilities are. The current preference for competencies is an attempt to put likely future skill needs into a developmental context, so that employees may see how they need to develop in order to meet them. But the transitions that will be needed, and hence the skill needs that will emerge, are often discovered too late. And even if we know that certain competencies are going to be in demand, it is another story entirely as to how to acquire them.

Rather, the information about the future which employees need **concerns the business** itself. What are the key issues which top management believes the business is facing and will face, and how is it intending to address them? Employees will then draw their own inferences about the probabilities of continued expansion, short-termism, devolution or whatever. And they will also infer the transitions that are likely to follow from these strategic directions. As Investors in People has recognized, full, accurate, and open information about the business is the most important thing that top management can tell employees. Organizations which have realized this do it in different ways:

- Hewlett Packard UK holds a regular open briefing meeting addressed by the CEO or his deputy.

- The CEO in Shell Chemicals UK used a video to brief staff on what the year's objectives were, and, a year later, on the extent to which they had been achieved.

- Almost every organization of any size has a company newspaper, but these differ in terms of their purpose – to enhance morale or to inform (although the two are not necessarily incompatible).

- The Department for Education and Employment holds a series of seminars on business issues open to all staff.

- The Post Office uses video screens in key places such as reception areas and canteens to announce results or significant business changes.

- Many now use e-mail for the same purpose.

INDIVIDUAL WANTS AND OFFERS

So employees should be aware of the present and future organizational needs for transitions to be made and skills to be acquired, so that they may know what it is that they should offer if they are to meet them. But, as arrow 3 in Figure 8.1 demonstrates, this is not the only information employees need in order to help them decide what they should offer the organization. They also need to inform themselves of what it is that they want and need as individuals. And this is not as easy as at first appears. We find it hard to take the time to ask ourselves such questions as:

- what our career anchor really is

- whether our circumstances have changed sufficiently to force us to reorder our priorities

- what our financial needs are at present and are likely to be in the future

- what are the pros and contras of, e.g. part-time working, or a cross-functional move
- what our personal overall sense of direction and life goals is
- how secure our self-esteem, our identity, and our sense of control are
- what we are good at, and hence what we enjoy doing.

Sun Microsystems

Sun Microsystems has recognized the need of its employees for in-depth career reviews from time to time. These take place outside the boss–subordinate appraisal system through a one-day career workshop. These are run every month, and 1,000 employees have attended them over the last three years. They help employees look at their personal values and possible career choices. After the workshop, a career discussion takes place with a manager of the employee's choice, and there is also follow-up by the HR function. Sun keeps itself aware of its employees' attitudes to career and other issues through a rolling sample survey.

KEY POINT

However, there is considerable difficulty in retaining the long-term perspective of career reviews. An international manufacturing organization devised a plan for holding career reviews at three crucial points in individuals' organizational career: after five years, at mid-career (age 35–40) and at late career (around 50). The idea behind these reviews was to exchange information and discover the other party's expectations, so that action could be taken if expectations did not match. Unfortunately, events overtook the plan. Staff started retiring or being retired much earlier, so the third point of review seemed unnecessary. The mid-career review proved very difficult to conduct meaningfully in the light of organizational and business changes and of the perceived danger of misunderstandings. The five-year-in review proved useful in structuring the early career experiences of recruits, but of course lost the long-term focus which was the original objective.

A pharmaceutical company assessed the reasons for attendance at its career workshop and the outcomes as perceived by the attendders. Given the opportunity of supplying one or more reasons for their attendance, 79 percent said they came to reassess their career decisions, 51 percent because they were dissatisfied with their present job, and 17 percent because they were dissatisfied with their private life. The most frequent outcomes were undertaking company-funded training (61 percent), making changes in their personal life (42 percent), making changes in their job content (34 percent), and actually changing job (29 percent).

Self-assessment along these dimensions is not easy. Some organizations provide career workshops to help individuals address these questions and relate the answers they come up with to what the organization wants.

A frequent alternative to such workshops is a development centre, which allows people to try out tasks taken from different jobs at different levels. This permits them to get a preview of different sorts of transition that they might make. It also helps them to discover how good they are at them, whether they enjoy them, and how they need to develop to do them better. Career workshops are likely to help employees address the

Bass

Bass has a development centre for graduate entrants who have completed their initial three-year training period, and also for other employees who have demonstrated high potential by their job performance. The process has been renamed an assessment centre, since it primarily performs a selection function. Its purpose is to determine who should enter the next stage of the management development programme, which consists of a series of tough cross-functional assignments.

As can be seen, however, the process is also developmental. Feedback is given to all on their strengths and weaknesses via counselling and 360° feedback, a personal development plan is constructed, and a mentor appointed. Both those who do and those who do not pass on to the next stage of the management development programme are expected to pursue their own personal development plan.

deeper and more personal issues, development centres the more job-related ones.

There are also several questionnaires and booklets which people have found useful, among them:

- Career Anchors (for discovering our fundamental career driver)[2]

- Career Concept Questionnaire (for understanding different transitions)[3]

- Strong-Campbell Interest Inventory (for understanding career interests)[4]

- Self-Directed Search (as Strong-Campbell Interest Inventory)[5]

- Work Locus of Control Scale (for estimating feeling of being in control)[6]

- Career Orientation Inventory (for understanding long-term career aims)[7]

- Life–Career Rainbow, (for working out our preferred work–life balance).[8]

Or we can just go and talk about it with our friends. But beware if they are work colleagues, since norms from the organization may obscure individual preferences and interests.

For many employees, the needs to earn a reliable living and to bring up a family are the two most important career drivers. Whatever the drivers are, however, and however basic or sophisticated they may be, employees cannot make transition offers unless they are aware of their needs. From fitting working periods to school holidays through to maintaining a professional identity despite cross-functional moves, these needs should inform what transition offers individuals make to their organization. There exists a variety of ways of helping employees become more aware of their needs; whatever method is used, such investigation has to occur repeatedly.

ORGANIZATIONAL OFFERS TO INDIVIDUALS

Exactly the same logic applies to the offers the organization makes to individuals (Figure 8.1, arrows 1 and 2). Not only does it need to know which transitions it wants employees to make, but also the needs of its employees in order to inform its offer to them. While organizations are often reasonably clear in their idea of what it is that they themselves want, they are not always so well informed as to the variety of wants of their employees. Indeed, they usually underestimate their diversity. This miscalculation actually handicaps them in their efforts to reconcile individuals' preferences with organizational requirements. For organizational labour flexibility requires a variety of employee transition preferences.

It is the problem of discovering what those preferences are that is the tough one, since it requires a degree of trust. Employees are not going to inform management that, for example, a shorter working week would suit their family needs particularly well at present, if they believe that the organization is likely to use that information to their disadvantage. They might fear that such an expression of their current need would cast doubts on their degree of commitment to the organization. Or they might simply anticipate that part-time status would result in their losing benefits attached to full-time work. If formal career workshops or self-assessment opportunities have been provided, it is usually and rightly the case that the information derived from these is private to and owned by the employee, so the organization cannot hope for information from that source. No, the organization has somehow got to devise a way of engendering sufficient trust to elicit employees' real needs from the horse's mouth.

One gradualist procedure to this end is to conduct anonymous surveys enabling the organization to estimate the numbers of those interested in making various transitions. In such a survey of middle managers in the finance sector,[9] one of the authors asked these questions (numbering is from the more extensive original questionnaire):

> How likely would you be to accept each of the following options
> if you were offered them tomorrow?
>
> 1 A promotion one level up (very unlikely, unlikely, possible, likely, very likely)
>
> 2 An assurance that you can stay in your present job until you retire
>
> 6 A move to another job at the same level
>
> 7 A move to join a project team

8   A move to a different business area

13   Early retirement

14   Voluntary redundancy on favourable terms

15   A part-time contract

17   A downward move with protected pension

19   A temporary move into another job

20   A secondment to another organization

22   More responsibility in your present job.

Responses suggested that most were unwilling to accept those transitions of which they had least experience. A summary of responses to such a questionnaire can enable organizations to discover the overall extent to which employee preferences match organizational needs. It can also demonstrate to individuals that there is a variety of options, and that all are attractive to at least some of their colleagues.

If the parties make their offers of transitions informed not only by their own needs and wants but also by those of the other, then those offers are more likely to be compatible. However, there is unlikely to be perfect correspondence, and negotiation/dialogue will have to occur. One of the major sources of employee organizational commitment is if the organization, even if it holds the labour market power, negotiates a career deal rather than imposes one. If its offers are well informed, it is unlikely to have to make major concessions anyway. More about negotiation in the next chapter.

WHAT IS THE TRANSITION LIKE?

Information is not only needed about what transitions are available and wanted, however, with the objective of negotiating appropriate transitional moves. It is also required about the nature of the transition itself, in order to help employees get up to speed fast and comfortably. Information will enable those making the transition to prepare, encounter and adjust better. Some ways of informing those making transitions in advance have already been explored (p. 115). We should also mention the use of videos, literature, and briefings about the job which describe it realistically: realistic job previews. The consequence of these is to reduce unrealistic expectations, and so decrease the amount of turnover which results when expectations are disappointed. Another benefit is that such previews enable one to see what the role involves, and rehearse how one might play it oneself: anticipatory socialization. The more the preview reveals how present role players feel about the job, the more complete the preparation, for one can imagine how one might feel oneself if the job arouses these feelings in others. If the impression is given that this is what it is going to be like anyway, like it or lump it, one may feel that there is going to be lit-

---

KEY POINT

One form of realistic job preview is a temporary secondment without prejudice. Such an arrangement removes the fear that there is no return ticket if the course does not become permanent. Some companies allow their staff to take on a small responsibility in a new area before leaving the old one. For example, a scientist could manage a small sales account before applying for a career move into the sales function. This gives both parties, the organization and the employee, a chance to evaluate the likely success of a significant career transition. International companies have for long had to deal with the return ticket problem. Unilever, for example, has a rigorous system for defining which part of the organization is responsible in career terms for each individual. Major transitions redefine this responsibility, but temporary assignments do not. Such a system gives employees the confidence to believe that they will not fall down ravines in the organizational structure if they take a temporary or risky job move.

---

tle chance of adjusting the role to oneself as well as vice-versa.[10]

FEELINGS MATTER

The balance between information about the task and the role demands and information about feelings and social relations is very important. On the one hand, research demonstrates that when people start a new role they are hungry for information about what they should be doing and what is required of them by way of skills and knowledge.[11] On the other hand, when it is investigated which sort of information leads them to be more satisfied with their job, perform better, and intend to stay, it is not technical or performance information. Rather, at least for a sample of American accountants, it is about expectations, norms and values, how to 'fit in'.[12] And the source of information that worked best was their own observation, rather than asking or reading.

This research finding forces us back to the **affective side** of transitions, the extent to which individuals feel that the transition is in accord with their values and their identity. It may be that adjustment is to an unavoidable change, and that identity and value priorities as well as behaviour may alter as a consequence. All the more reason why affective information should be conveyed as far as possible in advance, so that the individual can prepare themselves for personal as well as job change. And the most effective form of affective communication is self-acquired, where one has had the opportunity of seeing other people encountering and adjusting to the new role.

What does it feel like to go part time? Do people ever adjust to having been made redundant? Could I really take the pressure of a promotion? Would I find it greener on the other side of the fence? Will I feel guilty about going back to full-time work? Am I really a salesperson? Will I ever really like the sort of people who work there? Will they ever really like me? How much would I really have to change to fit in there? These questions can only be answered if people have the opportunity of seeing others at work in the new situation and imagining themselves in it; or, at second best, asking them about it. It is no accident that some organizations have started bringing back to the organization for a visit those who have received outplacement help during redundancy programmes and found another job. Others send recent graduate employees round to universities with instructions to answer honestly any question about what it is like to work for the company.

However, perhaps the most common feeling about transitions, especially during the preparation and encounter phases, is **uncertainty**. What exactly will happen? What help will I get? We have purposely not concentrated on managerial careers in this book, but here is a rarefied example from the very top of organizations: transition to the board:[13]

- Relatively few new board members have presented to the board before joining it, sat in on a board meeting, or met non-executive directors.

- Few have an identified mentor with whom they can discuss concerns, obtain coaching, and receive feedback. Some, but not many, chairmen perform this role.

- Many had their careers managed by the organization without their realizing it. Sometimes they only learned they were destined for higher things because they had to be given a reason for accepting a posting they were inclined to reject.

- The board and HR director, however, believe that the coming stars must somehow be aware of the fact that they are perceived to have the highest potential.

So the lack of communication in some cases is almost complete:

> I hadn't the faintest idea I was in the frame till they
> sent me off for a course on strategy.

Or where informative experience had been provided, it had not been helpful:

> You're put through the mill. It's like being attacked by
> the dogs. They're looking out for pitfalls all the
> time – a truly chilling experience. [presenting to the
> board]

Or perhaps this was merely a truly realistic job preview.

And while we are still in the organizational stratosphere, we should not forget those burdened at an early stage in their career with the label 'high potential'. Each of their speedy moves up the flattened pyramid is now going to involve a qualitative jump, often little smaller than the last leap up to the board. What do they know about each next level up and how are they to find out about it? Often the information is one-way only, to the top management; and that information is whether golden boy or girl has sunk or swum. As one of our respondents put it:

> The spotlight is on you; if you don't perform you're
> in trouble. They use difficult assignments to test the
> metal . . . survival of the fittest if you like.

It may be the case that organizations give little information to future board members because they think they are experienced enough not to need it. However, we suspect that there is often little provided to those lower down the hierarchy in terms of what transitions may be in store for them and how they might best prepare for the encounter and adustment phases. Why?

The answer is that organizations provide career information for a wide variety of reasons:

- They may want to get as wide a field as possible for vacancies, so they install a job posting system.

- They may want to justify a round of redundancies, so they give a full financial account to employees.

- They may want to improve morale, so they present a selection of good news items.

- They may want to retain able and ambitious people, so they indicate possible promotional paths.

Once again we can see that these are all perfectly reasonable short- or medium-term career management objectives. However, they do not embrace the radical rethink implied by career contracting. If organizations are to follow the career contracting model, information will not be one-way. Rather it will be a dialogue, with each party informing the other of its wants and offers. For it is only when wants and offers have been made explicit that contracting can occur. Thus organizations will need to:

- get from employees, as well as give them, transition-related inform-ation; this will also require organizations to provide individuals with the chance to gain information about their own needs in order to give it to the organization

- give the information that employees need in order to formulate their transition offers; this will include current opportunities for making transitions, business directions, skills needed, etc.

- give information that helps employees in the preparation, encounter, and adjustment phases, including feedback about their success at each of these stages

- get information back from employees during these phases so as to help them more effectively to negotiate successfully.

A wide variety of HR processes is available to help achieve these aims and to enable development to occur. Some have already been mentioned in this chapter, but for the sake of completeness, we can list them using five different functions which they perform in order to categorize them:

1 Assessment of skills, knowledge, anchors, interests, etc.
   - appraisal, 360° feedback, questionnaires, psychometrics, assessment centres.

2 Identification of options
   - development centres, job maps, competency frameworks, information interview.

3 Action planning
   - self-help packages, courses, workshops, counselling, mentoring, PDPs.

4 Skill development
   - learning centres, external qualifications, training.

5 Job access
   - vacancy filling, job rotation, succession planning, secondments.

Information is crucial to the contracting process and therefore to the management of career transitions in general. Yet again, however, we have to admit that the whole process of exchanging information is pointless in the absence of trust. For without trust, employees will not believe the information the organization gives them, nor will they trust it with theirs.

Some questions to think about

1 To what extent does your organization inform employees what transitions it is likely to want them to make, and where it believes the business is heading? What formal processes are in place to help it do so, and how effective are they?

2 To what extent does your organization help employees discover their own transition preferences, and to what extent does it elicit these from them? What formal processes are in place for these purposes if any, and how effective are they?

3 To what extent does your organization inform employees in advance about the transition itself, the process of making the transition, the nature of the new role? Does it use any form of realistic job preview, or other such processes? How effective are they?

REFERENCES

1 Hirsh, W. and Jackson, C. (1996) 'Strategies for career development: promise, practice, and pretence'. Brighton: Institute for Employment Studies, Report 305.
2 Schein, E.H. (1990) *Career Anchors: Discovering Your Real Values*. San Diego: Pfeffer.
3 Driver, M. and Brousseau, K. (1981) *The Career Concept Questionnaire*. Los Angeles: Decision Dynamics Corporation.
4 Hansen, J.C. and Campbell, D.P. (1985) *Manual for the SVIB SCII*, 4th edn. Palo Alto, CA: Consulting Psychologists Press.
5 Holland, J.L. (1985) *The Self-Directed Search: Professional Manual*. Odessa, FL: Psychological Assessment Resources.
6 Spector, P.E. (1988) 'Development of the work locus of control scale'. *Journal of Occupational Psychology* 61: 335–40.
7 Jansen, E. and Chandler, G. (1989) *Career Orientation Inventory*. Utah: University of Utah.
8 Super, D.E. (1980) 'A life-span, life-space approach to career development'. *Journal of Vocational Behaviour* 16: 282–98.
9 Herriot, P., Pemberton, C. and Hawtin, E. (1996) 'The career attitudes and intentions of managers in the finance sector'. *British Journal of Management* 7: 181–90.
10 Arnold, J. (1997) *Managing Careers into the 21st Century*. London: Paul Chapman.
11 Ostroff, C. and Kozlowski, S.W.J. (1993) 'Organisational socialisation as a learning process: the role of information acquisition'. *Journal of Vocational Behaviour* 42: 170–83.
12 Morrison, E.W. (1993) 'Longitudinal study of the effects of information seeking on newcomer socialisation'. *Journal of Applied Psychology* 78: 173–83.
13 Pemberton, C. and Herriot, P. (1995) *Getting on Board: The Development of Directors*. London: Careers Research Forum.

Managing transitions 9

If careers are sequences of transitions, then the task of career management is to manage those transitions. There are four fundamental tasks of career transition management:

- to ensure that the career transitions individuals are asked to make match the business transitions which the organization is making; are they the right ones and at the right time?

- to decide which transitions it is appropriate to ask different categories of employee, or different employees within those categories, to make, and what support to offer them

- to so manage the career contracting process that both parties' needs are met as far as is possible

- to so manage the transition process itself that each stage is an adequate platform for the next, enabling individuals to adjust successfully and rapidly.

We will review each of these management tasks in turn.

THE RIGHT PEOPLE IN THE RIGHT PLACE AT THE RIGHT TIME

We described in Chapter 5 the types of career transition that match the six phases of organizational change, and subsequently described some of the HR systems that support them. Table 9.1 summarizes these phases and systems.

It is not too difficult, then, to design coherent sets of processes to support the career transitions which are implied by the six different organizational change phases. We must remember that only three of the six will be in phase at any one point in time. Of course, it may be much more

Organizational change phase	Dominant career transition	Support HR processes
Growth	• Role change, promotion • Into the Organization • Into project teams	• External training, development workshops • Induction programmes • Recruitment drives
Contraction	• Role enlargement • Heavier workloads • Out of the organization	• Performance management • Wage constraint • Outplacement
Long term	• Developmental moves • Cross-functional moves • Moves within the organization	• Competency analysis • Resourcing plans • Personal development plans • Potential assessment • Career workshops
Short term	• Best people into the job • Temporary jobs • Into and out of the organization	• Training on and for the job • Performance assessment • Skill pools • Rapid recruitment
Devolution	• Into more generalist jobs • Within business moves • Within locality moves	• Local HR consultants • Line manager training • Locally tailored personnel systems
Centralization	• Into specialist jobs • Across business moves • Between locality moves	• Corporate talent pools • Succession planning • Corporate information systems

Table 9.1 Organizational change, career transitions and HR processes

difficult to introduce them and make them actually work – design is usually easier than implementation.

However, as we have argued throughout, most organizations do not
stay consistently within one phase, nor is the whole organization always
at the same point in the cycle. Those that do stay in one phase are often
those expanding, long-term organizations which are held up as models
of HR practice. It would be nice to assume that their success is due to
their use of the appropriate HR processes. Unfortunately, the research
seems to show that HR virtue follows more often than it precedes business success.[1][2] The path of by far the majority of larger organizations is
much less smooth. They may change from any one end of any of the three
dimensions to its opposite as a consequence of changes in their business
environment or leadership. Hence the benchmarks of excellence held up
to them in management texts and magazines may not meet their business needs. They may merely serve to make them despondent. Rather,
these organizations need to consider what forms of career management
might conceivably help them change from asking for certain transitions
and using certain HR processes to asking for and using quite different
ones. Oceanic turbulence necessitates changing tack for most.

Effects of changes in tack

To demonstrate how major the effects of such changes of tack may be,
consider the following organizational transitions:

- From **growth to contraction**, where the strategic emphasis has probably changed from innovation and improved quality to cost control and
  enhanced productivity.

- From **long- to short-termism**, where opportunism and flexibility as
  opposed to planning and mission are now the aims.

- From **devolution to centralization**, where freedom to take certain decisions locally is now being drawn back to the corporate centre.

Each of these changes of tack implies that different sorts of **career transitions** dominate:

- Sudden contraction after growth will mean greater use of agencies or outsourcing, or the creation of bigger or part-time jobs, instead of recruitment
  aplenty, promotions, and job moves. Gone are the external training courses, and in their place are powerful performance assessment and controls.

- When short-termism takes over, the people who are best at a job will be moved to it or kept in it. Promised developmental moves are suddenly off the agenda, and people may be told they are only in a job for as long as necessary and provided they perform – a far cry from a secure internal labour market.

- A sudden pull back to central control implies similar radical changes in transitions. Moves to corporate HQ and specialist jobs will suddenly interrupt a local career in a single business. Corporate allocation of people to positions will replace the line manager's decisions and patronage, and local HR information systems will be drawn into the centre.

The era of just-in-time management is nigh

And of course, the reverse changes will happen if the tack is changed in the opposite direction to these three examples. How can HR managers possibly succeed in reversing policies and practices in time to enable career transitions to coincide with business ones? The era of just-in-time career management is upon us. Here are several things that they can do to make it a reality:

1 Read the organization's business transition phases accurately: are we moving towards a phase change or away from one? Has growth eased off? Are we just starting to think long term? Is the zeal to delegate everything burning itself out as its limitations are beginning to be felt? Or, contrariwise, are we seeing expansionary light at the end of the tunnel? Is a sudden merger forcing us to think only for the present? Are we finding the organization too unwieldy to be amenable to central control any more?

2 Use scenario and contingency planning to open people's minds to different future possibilities and to the varying implications of these for resources and skills.

3 Manage employees' expectations accordingly. Then the reversal of some HR policies and practices is seen as a necessary consequence of the reversal of the business direction, rather than as a breaking of a deal by management.

4 Use career management systems which are capable of use in both phases. Fast-track cohorts, for example, are suited only to the long-term and centralized phases of the cycles, whereas the assessment of knowledge, skills and aptitudes is going to be of use whatever the phase the

organization is in. While newly required knowledge and skills may not be immediately available in the organization, it is possible that just-in-time training could prove quicker, less expensive, and have better consequences for morale than redundancies and predominantly external recruitment.

5 Ensure that the employees and the organization are willing, and indeed expect, to renegotiate the career contract periodically. If the deal has already been renegotiated because employees' wants have changed, then employees are more likely to accept its renegotiation when the same is true of the organization. Nevertheless, if the change of tack is, for example, from long- to short-termism, this will not be easy. For such a change implies a change in the very nature of the deal, from a relationship to a transaction.

6 Have as one of the aims of every form of development an increase in the capacity to make transitions and to support others in making them.

SOME ARE MORE EQUAL THAN OTHERS: MANAGING THE ALLOCATION OF TRANSITIONS

In response to the pressures for flexibility, some organizations have developed very different career deals for different types of employee. The full range of career deals, together with the development deals that support them, can be seen in Figure 9.1. Our recent research[3] has demonstrated that there are some organizations where every one of these career and development deals are present simultaneously. These organizations have clearly bought their labour flexibility by **segmenting** employees as though, in effect, different categories of employee are working in different organizations. What is more, they have also bought the capacity to adjust to external labour markets, for they can offer the best career deals, if necessary, to those whose skills and knowledge are in short supply.

Other organizations have sought to avoid such segmentation, and it is interesting to note that they are those which have recognized the importance of operatives or shopfloor staff to the business. Such companies as Rover, Marks and Spencer, and John Lewis emphasize the single status of all employees, and some even signal this by a common dress uniform across all levels of the hierarchy. Their aim is to enhance organizational commitment and good corporate citizenship as a consequence of perceptions of common fate and equity. However, we should note that such unified deals are just as likely to have been imposed by top management as

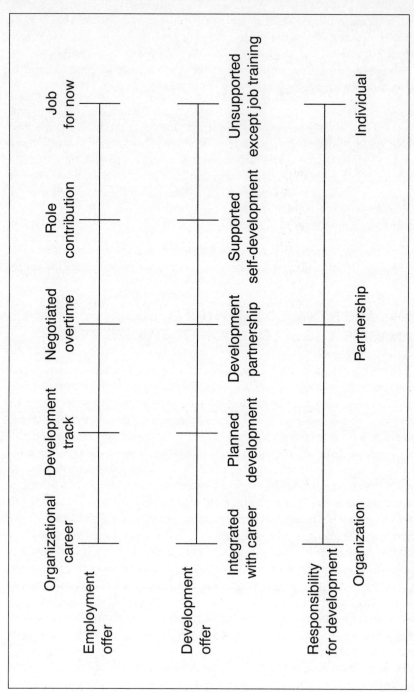

Figure 9.1   The range of deals

is the segmentation described; and that these organizations tend to hold a unitarist rather than a pluralist view of organizational interests.

What will be appropriate in the future?

That is why neither segmented nor unified career and development deals are going to be appropriate in the future. If the process of individual career contracting is going to be a necessary and central condition for successful employment relationships, then both solutions are mistaken. For both relate to categories of staff (or the whole workforce); and both are likely to have been decided for them. It may well be the case that there is a strong relationship between category of employee and employee wants and needs. As we have noted, it is entirely to be expected that managerial staff will have a managerial career anchor and professional employees a technical/functional or an autonomy one. Many operatives and office staff will have a security, lifestyle or service anchor, and so on. This is hardly surprising, since they will mainly have self-selected into those categories which suit their anchors. Alternatively, the rewards and lifestyle which some enjoy enable them to satisfy their anchors, whereas those further down the hierarchy have to concentrate on meeting more immediate needs.

However, it does not follow that the wants and offers of all employees in a particular category are the same, although it is convenient for HR systems and practice to assume that they are. On the contrary, there are many at the operative level who, for example, have ambitions to manage and the potential to do so. There are also many in the middle management and professional ranks for whom security and lifestyle are anchors. If individual career contracts are negotiated, then there is far greater labour flexibility available to organizations than if they are segmented by category. For many of the requirements for flexibility of labour supply or of employee skills are within particular employee categories.

Many operatives or telesales staff, for example, are anxious for a career deal which meets their lifestyle needs; others want to remain full time for reasons of security. Such a division of preferences matches the organization's need for shift working to support a 24-hour service. Organizational and individual needs can both be met, but only if the organization has undertaken an individual career contracting process. Exactly the same is true of people higher up the hierarchy. Those with a technical/professional anchor or a perceived need to remain employable externally, may seek to remain in a functional path. Others with a strong managerial or pure challenge anchor may seek a cross-functional move. Again, these preferences are likely to match the flatter structure of organizations in which fewer managerial positions are available.

Problems with segmentation

Segmentation without reference to individual differences in wants and offers within each segment has two other major drawbacks. First, if wants differ, then the imposition of a single deal within a segment will fail to motivate many of the employees within that segment. And second, a lot of potential talent will be lost. For one characteristic of segmented organizations is that it is remarkably difficult and rare to move from one segment to another.[4] This means that a lot of talented people are going to be unable to express that talent in the segment to which it is most suited. No organization will be able to afford not to use to the full all the talent at its disposal, as Bass and ICL have recognized in their efforts to support cross-segment moves.

There are other problems with blatant segmentation:

- Feelings of inequity arise constantly, particularly if the organization is unwise enough to engage in rhetoric of the 'common fate, all one big happy family' variety.

- Major resourcing difficulties arise if it suddenly becomes necessary to increase or decrease numbers in one or another of the segments. Given the difficulty of transferring employees successfully from one segment to another, organizations have to declare redundancies within a segment, or recruit externally into it. If other organizations are seeking to do the same and there is a seller's labour market, then this will be an expensive option.

- If some of the segments consist of agency employees, short-term contract employees, or outsourced workers, then the resourcing links with the core can be severed.

- A multiplicity of HR processes is required if there are different career deals operating in different segments.

Flexibility and motivation are better achieved by career contracting with individuals than by either segmentation or single status.

MANAGING THE CONTRACTING PROCESS

The third task of career management is to manage the career contracting process. The initial task here is to decide how the general principles of the career contracting process depicted in Figure 6.1 and described on pp. 100–101 are to be put into practice in a particular situation in a specific organization. For there is a wide range of possible actualizations of these principles in practice:

- A first-level supervisor might hold informal conversations with his or her subordinates on learning that an extension of the service which they offer is being planned.

- Project teams may plan together for the transition from their present major project, which they see coming to an end, to several smaller ones.

- Members of the pool of the top 200 in the corporation may have initial confidential discussions with the personnel director on learning the identity of the new CEO and his or her likely leadership style and direction.

We do not believe, however, that it is a managerial task to establish the principles of career contracting as organizational policy and practice. This, we will argue in Chapter 10, is a leadership rather than a managerial responsibility. Managers need to work out how to express the principles in their neck of the woods.

Implementation

Managing the contracting process also involves making sure that it happens in some form or another. This issue of implementation is consistently ignored. It is far more interesting and career enhancing to formulate policies, introduce initiatives, and design systems than it is to make sure that something happens on the ground. HR gurus and repeated conferences concern themselves with the former, but questioning of the internal clients often reveals huge gaps between theory and practice.[5] It is therefore not surprising that several of the biggest management consultancies make their living from implementation rather than strategy. Yet there can be no more immediate or important task than ensuring that the right people actually are in the right place at the right time in an era when the times themselves are changing ever faster.

There are several possible explanations for this theory–practice gap:

- Bottom-line short-term targets dominate managers' thinking and action in many organizations.

- Many line managers are ill equipped and ill motivated to manage the career contracting process.

- It is often counter to their own interests to help their best people make a transition.

- Authority to do local career deals (within parameters) has not been delegated.

- Career contracting has not been embedded into the organizational change process, so managers see no business reason to carry it through.

- Career transitions are seen as closely tied to the economic cycle, and therefore inevitable.

- Transitions have been imposed rather than negotiated, so there is no motivation to make them work.

The elements of career contracting

Nevertheless, if career contracting is to be managed on the ground so that it actually occurs, how will that happen? We have already described in Chapter 8 some of the ways of ensuring information exchange, the first element of the process (see Figure 6.1). There are the other three elements to consider, however: negotiation or dialogue, monitoring and exit or renegotiation.

Negotiation

One issue about negotiation is who represents the parties. One of the common facts of organizational life is that different messages come from different representatives. Line managers may encourage only local transitions, while HR managers may expect cross-business and cross-locality mobility. Which broker of the organization's needs should I deal with, wonders the employee? Who has the power to fulfil any promises they may make? How do we reconcile local business and central corporate needs, thinks top management? The CEO will have to bang their heads together. So who represents the organization?

Likewise with the employee. Who is to represent their career interests in career contracting? If it is to be their union or staff association, how willing are these to do individual rather than collective deals on behalf of their members? Yet if the employee contracts on his or her own behalf, there are difficult issues of power. Employees may, for example, have labour market power on their side if they are offering scarce knowledge and skills. Yet this asset may be negated by their lack of personal power and skill in negotiating, or by their lack of a union, patron, mentor, or agent to support their case.

A fundamental managerial skill in the contracting process is to have enabled the parties to have acquired and exchanged so much relevant information that each understands the limited range of transition offers which the other finds it possible to make. But there will inevitably be conflicts of interest, and power is likely to determine the favourability of outcome for each party. What is important is that inequality of power does not tempt the party who enjoys the upper hand to forgo the contracting process entirely. Throughout the last decade and a half, organizations have tended to enjoy labour market power, and as a consequence to impose rather than negotiate career transition 'deals'. They are only now realizing the dangers of such unilateral imposition as employees without labour market power keep their heads down, while those now with it respond in kind.

As a City trader recently said:

> I made 12 million for you yesterday. Give me a million of it, or I'm off tomorrow.

Monitoring

The next stage of the contracting process is that of monitoring the deal. Once each party's offers have been accepted by the other, what happens next? The first monitoring task is to ensure that the transitions that have been agreed are actually happening – back to the implementation issue. The only way to discover whether they are is to hold a meeting between the two contracting parties, the organizational representative and the individual and/or their representative. Such meetings should have been built into the contract so that they are timed to check up on a key point in the transition process:

- Has your part-time duty roster been designed as agreed so as to fit in with school holidays?

- Did the promised training course to enable you to change function occur as planned?

- Is the agreement as to the number of hours you should work part time being kept, or are you already under pressure to work what is in effect a full working week for part-time money?

But that is only part of the monitoring stage. **Equity** is always an issue in career contracting, and it is important to check that the deal is perceived as fair. Otherwise, employees lose respect for and commitment to the organization,[6] and take their own measures to restore the equity balance unofficially.

The factor which has the greatest effect on perceptions of equity is the identity of the comparison.[7] With whose deal am I comparing my own? The usual answer has been that I think of the balance between what certain other people contribute and what they receive, and then compare that ratio with my own. Hence if I see, for example, directors receiving huge golden handshakes as they leave the organization, I may speculate on the contribution which they have or have not made to justify such treatment. I then think of my own contribution, and compare the likely pay-off I will get if I am made redundant.

Two features of career contracting make it less likely that equity comparisons will take the same form as hitherto. First, most comparisons have usually been about the relative contribution that different jobs make to the organization's success, and indeed a whole industry of job evaluation has been built upon this fact. Now, however, it will be transitions rather than jobs that are being negotiated. The contribution comes more from making the change effectively than from performing in the rare stabilization phase of a career transition. So comparisons will be more with what sorts of transitions other people are making. Second, deals will become more individually tailored than collectively uniform. Hence there will ultimately be differences in deals all over the place. Initially, individualization of career contracts will result in more perceptions of inequity because more comparisons are possible. However, ultimately people may compare their present deal with their own previous one, not always unfavourably. What is certain is that nothing exceeds the degree of inequity felt by those in a highly segmented organization who are fed a rhetoric of family, equality and the importance of people to the busines.[8] The management and monitoring of perceived equity is a fundamental element of the contracting process.

Finally, monitoring is required of organizational and individual needs. We have already noted the importance of anticipating changes of tack in the organization's course. The same is equally true of individuals. And just as the organizational changes are more frequent and less predictable, so the changes of tack in our own lives have often lost that stereotypical sequence of life stages that we used to use to help us make sense of them . . . if they ever had it in reality. Now we are often parents and children simultaneously for long periods, and many of us acquire more of both of these blessings at unexpected intervals.

Of course one can simply state that there should be periodic meetings with line managers to monitor whether personal needs have changed, but systems are not a sufficient answer. It is only when there is sufficient trust in the organization that employees do not feel that advantage will be taken of their statement of changed personal needs that any such disclosure is likely. Some few organizations in the UK (but over 80 percent of Fortune 500 companies in the USA) use employee assistance programmes.[9] However, the confidentiality which is of the essence in such externally provided services is likely to prevent the individual employee's changed needs from getting onto their career contracting agenda. No, there is no substitute for mutual trust in an organization which embraces and acts out the career contracting model and values.

Renegotiation or exit

Finally, renegotiation or exit are the alternative next stages to be managed. There are two fundamental managerial decisions to be taken at this point of the model. The first is this: how big does the violation of the contract have to be, how unfair does it now have to seem, how much do parties' needs have to have changed, before this final stage is triggered? Putting it another way, how strong does the answer 'no' have to be to the questions of the monitoring stage in Figure 6.1 before we have to take action? Many organizations seem to pick up rapidly the equity issues while failing to note changes in their own or their employees' needs until the whole deal is at risk.

The second decision is whether to go for renegotiation or exit. Can we use this employee in a different role, or should we make him or her redundant, is a frequent and difficult question. Whatever the answer, the manner of exit is a statement about the culture and values of the organization. The management of exit has huge implications for the morale of the remaining employees, the attitude of customers and the reputation of the company.[10]

MANAGING THE TRANSITION ITSELF

Which brings us on to the fourth and last of the fundamental tasks of managing career transitions: managing the transition process itself. We have already suggested that the traditional division of transitions into the four stages of preparation, encounter, adjustment and stabilization is typically now truncated into the first three of these only. And we have already noted various processes that can prove useful at each of these stages. Realistic job previews, for example, can help during the preparation stage (see p. 140); induction and on-the-job training are often useful during adjustment (see p. 118).

The fundamental principle in managing transitions, however, is simple. It is that **the effective negotiation of subsequent stages depends on the adequacy of previous stages**.[11] If adequate preparation has not occurred, encounter will be a rude shock, the reaction to which may jeopardize relationships with new colleagues, and adjustment will be a matter of complete trial and error. If adequate preparation and encounter have not occurred, efforts at adjustment may be misplaced and badly received by new colleagues and boss. If adjustment of self to the role and role to the self is lacking or incomplete, performance will fail to get up to speed as soon as expected.

So we need to ask whether the employee in transition has had:

- a realistic job preview
- a recent history of their new department/work group
- contact with the existing job holder
- contact with future colleagues
- training targeted at the new job
- an induction programme if the organization or department is new to the individual
- allocation of a friend or mentor
- rapid and frequent feedback about encounter and adjustment successes and failures

- on-the-job training from the beginning.

All of these simple and inexpensive measures can help employees get up to speed faster, and thus improve productivity as transitions become more frequent. More deeply, some of them can give individuals a little help in dealing with the profound emotional effects of some transitions. Yet transition management is appallingly neglected in most organizations. We are so eager to engage in strategic thinking about careers in relation to the business, and the development of talent to that end, that we cannot see the most immediate and obvious ways in which we could have an impact here and now.

So much for the management of career transitions. The final chapter discusses what we believe will be the most fundamental requirement of all: leadership. Yet the importance of leadership in career transitions has not been recognized at all hitherto. Rather, career management has been treated as a technical task for the HR function.

Some questions to think about

1. Are the transitions which the organization requires of its employees compatible with the business phase in which it finds itself? What resourcing processes does it use to ensure that they are? Are they in place in time, or do they lag behind business transition? If so, why?

2. How segmented is your organization? How easy is it to move from one segment to another? How many administrative staff, for example, have become line managers? How aware are employees of the degree of segmentation in the organization?

3. How well does the organization manage the career contracting process overall? How coherent is it, and are the responsibilities for carrying it out clear? If the responsibility has been given to the line, has it the skills to do it properly?

4. How well does the organization manage the career transition process itself? Does it do so in a coherent way which recognizes the importance of the preparation stage as the foundation for subsequent ease of transition? Are transitions monitored in terms of time up to speed in the new job, employee satisfaction, new line manager's satisfaction, etc.? When employees leave, how often is it because job moves are not managed well? Do you know this from exit interviews?

REFERENCES

1. Hendry, C. and Pettigrew, A. (1992) 'Patterns of strategic change in the development of human resource management'. *British Journal of Management* 3 (3): 137–56.
2. Sisson, K. and Storey, J. (1993) *Managing Human Resources and Industrial Relations*. Milton Keynes: Open University Press.
3. Hirsh, W. and Jackson, C. (1996) 'Strategies for career development: promise, practice, and pretence'. Brighton: Institute for Employment Studies, Report 305.
4. Baron, J.N., Davis-Blake, A. and Bielby, W.T. (1986) 'The structure of opportunity: how promotion ladders vary within and among organisations'. *Administrative Science Quarterly* 31: 248–73.
5. Legge, K. (1995) *Human Resource Management: Rhetorics and Realities*. London: Macmillan.
6. McFarlin, D.B. and Sweeney, P.D. (1992) 'Distributive and procedural justice as predictors of satisfaction with personal and organisational outcomes'. *Academy of Management Journal* 35 (3): 626–37.
7. Adams, J.S. (1963) 'Towards an understanding of inequity'. *Journal of Abnormal and Social Psychology* 67: 422–36.
8. Legge, K. (1995) *Human Resource Management: Rhetorics and Realities*. London: Macmillan.
9. Midgley, S. (1997) 'Pressure points'. *People Management* 3 (1): 36–9.
10. Doherty, N. and Horsted, J. (1995) 'Redundancy management: helping survivors to stay on board'. *People Management* 1 (1): 26–31.
11. Nicholson, N. and West, M.A. (1988) *Managerial Job Change: Men and Women in Transition*. Cambridge: Cambridge University Press.

Leadership, trust and transitions

10

INTRODUCTION

We have to confess at this late stage that the title of our book is misleading. For it refers to the management of the employment relationship. Alert readers will have appreciated from the start that, despite the book's introduction, we were not about to write a treatise on global circumnavigation. However, it must have become ever clearer throughout the book that we are not primarily concerned with the management of careers either. If the two central ideas of the book are trust and transition, then any successful way of addressing these issues has to concentrate upon leadership as well as upon management. For such issues are not in the ultimate analysis primarily to do with managing people and processes; they are about relationships and mutual support through change.

Another brief recapitulation of the argument so far will clarify this assertion. We have proposed that mutual trust is a fundamental component of social capital without which voluntary collaboration in organizations is impossible. We produced evidence that the fund of social capital in western societies has decreased, both at a societal and at an organizational level. This loss, we argued, is exacerbated by the feelings of insecurity currently prevalent at most levels of society. Yet at such a point in time when trust is in short supply, the need for it in organizations has never been greater. This is because of the increased frequency of business transitions that most organizations are forced to undertake in the face of seemingly irresistible environmental changes. These business transitions involve changes in the structure of organizations, which in turn necessitate personal transitions on the part of employees. Some of these transitions may bring with them welcome opportunity and variety, but many are perceived as threats. These threats are directed both at employees' physical and at their psychological well-being.

In the second part of the book we have gone on to argue that personal transitions cannot be imposed as if they were merely an unimportant element of business change. Rather, a recognition is required that employees, too, have needs, which such transitions may or may not meet. Hence the only framework within which transitions may be successfully made is likely to be one of contracting rather than of imposition. We then went into some detail about how organizations' needs for flexibility could be reconciled with individuals' varied needs, so that the transitions made could serve both parties' interests. We emphasized that training and development were now for transitions rather than for stable jobs, recognizing that development had to help people cope with changes that affected them deeply. We then went into some detail about the need for clear communications if career contracting is to occur successfully, so we reviewed forms of information exchange. Finally, believing that the management of career transitions is fundamental to business success, we laid responsibility for that management onto senior managers in the organization. They must concern themselves with the management of the contracting process, and the management of career transitions themselves.

However, the issue of trust keeps recurring. For career contracting requires trust if it is to work. People who make agreements with each other need at the very least to believe that the other will keep its side of the deal. The only contracts which do not require trust are those where the likely contingencies and the penalties for violation are spelled out in such detail that the parties feel that no-one would dare to break them. That is emphatically not the case in the process of career contracting as we have described it. If it were, the transaction costs would be insupportable. Rather, mutual trust is required, not only to enable career contracting to occur, but also to bring confidence that the parties will support each other in the transitions which organization and individual must repeatedly make.

We will argue in this final chapter that the only way in which such a degree of trust can be recovered in organizations is through the exercise of leadership. We will risk renewed accusations of pessimism and cynicism by expanding on the reasons as to why trust was lost through an absence of leadership in the first place. But our purpose in so doing is to point up the need for different forms of leadership in the future. For unless such new leadership is forthcoming, people will not be willing to make the transitions necessary for the survival of organizations.

WHY HAS TRUST BEEN LOST?

In Chapter 2 we outlined the nature of trust in organizations. In brief we argued that trust involved believing that:

- others would act competently in their role

- they would be open and honest, not seeking to deceive

- they would not take advantage of me but rather be concerned for my welfare

- they would be reliable, behaving consistently and doing what they said they were going to do.

These elements of trust are interdependent.[1] If a person falls down in one of them, it is likely to damage my view of him or her as trustworthy, even though the other three elements are all present and correct. So, for example, I may not get a reputation for being trustworthy if I am so brutally honest that I damage colleagues by telling them exactly what I think of them. While I have been open and honest to a fault, I have failed to be concerned for their welfare. Or I may perform so competently in my job that I win a large performance-related bonus, but if I have done so at the expense of my subordinates' well-being or by breaking promises I will not be regarded as trustworthy overall.

However, a person is not judged trustworthy solely on the basis of what they have done. The perception of trustworthiness also derives from the motives or reasons we attribute to their actions.[2] Why, we ask, did she really do that? Was it because of:

- her role – someone in that position has to do that sort of thing?

- the situation – she had no choice in the matter, there was only one course of action possible?

- she is that sort of person – she usually has this or that motive uppermost in her mind?

Obviously all sorts of factors will affect such conclusions, not least our previous experience of her and our knowledge of her reputation with others. One such factor is her dealings with me. If she treats me without respect, then I can make three sorts of judgement as to her motives. It could be that:

1 She had every right to do so as my boss, since I deserved to be chewed off.

2 She had no choice because she was being leaned on herself to treat me so.

3 She had bad intentions towards me.

Given my need to preserve my self-esteem, and in the absence of a clear situational reason, I am apt to make the personal attribution: she dislikes me/is jealous of me/is a petty-minded bureaucrat etc.

If, however, she treats me with dignity and respect, my attributions may well be the opposite to these. Research indicates[3] that it is not so much what the outcomes are for me that matters. Rather, it is how the action was carried out: procedural rather than distributive justice. The amount of my performance-related pay is of little importance compared to the equity of the allocation and the feeling that I am being valued. And therein lies the nub. For if I am dealt with well, in a way that demonstrates dignity and respect, I believe I am valued. I am likely to maintain my self-esteem and at the same time attribute worthy reasons to the organization's agent.

KEY POINT

A recent industrial dispute in the UK exemplifies the importance of procedural equity. An employee said anonymously to a newspaper:[4]

> The whole thing stinks. When they claim on television that they haven't been intimidating us, it makes you laugh. I've kept all the threatening letters, video and audio tapes they've sent us and I've got a six inch file.

Another anonymous employee said to another newspaper:[5]

> [The company] is doing everything it said it would not do. After all the intimidation and threats we are being punished again.

We have already reviewed in Chapter 2 how many top managements have lost trustworthiness over recent times. They have demonstrated by their behaviour that:

- they are not always as competent as employees expect them to be
- they have not always been open, preferring rhetoric to honesty
- they have not demonstrated themselves to be concerned about employees' interests and well-being

- they have made promises which they have not been able, or sometimes willing, to keep.

Some have dragged down their overall trustworthiness rating by their failure in one respect, even though in other areas they have succeeded in their appallingly difficult task. Some top managements have skilfully engineered the financial survival of their organizations during recession, deserving a high rating for competence. But they are not perceived as trustworthy because part of their survival strategy required them to deceive employees as to the nature of their business intentions. Others were very open about the need for redundancies and the collapse of the notion of jobs for life, but they treated those they made redundant without dignity or respect. So the sources of trust are interrelated, and their overall impact on trustworthiness is crucial.

Sometimes employees have attributed motives to top management when attribution to the business situation might have been more reasonable. But perhaps such personal attributions occurred because the business case had not been put clearly or honestly. Or perhaps employees delighted in putting the worst possible construction on management decisions because of some other utterly crass action on the part of top management, such as awarding themselves huge salary rises in recession. This in itself will have served to decrease trustworthiness, and hence made derogatory personal attributions more likely. For how can they possibly be concerned for us, or for that matter for the company itself, employees reason, if they pay themselves a fortune while making us redundant?

The overall judgement has to be that while some loss of trust was inevitable in the business changes of the last few years, some top managements have made the situation worse by acting in ways which have decreased their own trustworthiness. Why have they done so? We have two explanations, one an external attribution, the other an internal one.

The perceived role of top management

Our external explanation rests upon the perceived role of top management. The idea that the primary role of top management is to take strategic business decisions is fundamental to our western business culture.[6] We assume that business (by which we mean financial) criteria are the most important ones to take into account, and we pay more attention to the expectations of certain stakeholders (e.g. shareholders) than we do to others (e.g. employees). These priorities are maintained in our ways of referring to human resources, a function which is directed to serving the business needs of the corporation. It is construed as the task of HR to devise ways of helping the business to achieve its (financial) objectives. The justification for this set of priorities is that if you do not make a profit you cannot employ people in the first place. A more formal way of expressing this justification is to say that financial viability is a necessary condition for organizational survival. We would argue that it is also a necessary condition for survival to have employees who are willing and able to make the career transitions that the situation requires.

The personality of top management

Our internal explanation for the decrease in trustworthiness of top management is based on the personality of top managers themselves. The most insightful accounts of the sort of person likely to finish up at the top of organizations are not based on those famous lists of traits that every leader must possess. Rather, they are more concerned with the types of motivation such people have, and how they cope with them.[7][8]

Many top managers have a healthy degree of self-esteem, which is sustained by the power, status, and prestige of their office, and the respect and admiration that often go with them. They are able to attribute their achievement to a mixture of opportunity and ability, and feel secure in their view of themselves as worthwhile people of some substance.

Others, however, are insecure in their self-esteem. They may perceive a threat to their power and position from others in the organization, whom they believe to be envious of them. Or they may lack the confidence in their own ability to match up to the incredible demands of the job. The very power which they feel is so threatened enables them to erect several powerful defences against these often imaginary threats, as follows:

- They can command admiration from followers who need to identify with power so as to feel they are sharing it themselves.

- They may treat any criticism or deviance as a personal attack; they may then create scapegoats of the deviants and turn them over to their followers to be humiliated.

- They may distance themselves from others in order to minimize the risk of being damaged.

- They may fear the success of others since it reflects badly on them, consequently tolerating mediocrity and avoiding stars.

- They may seek to control everything so that nothing can get out of control and harm them.

While top managers with secure self-esteem may inspire trust in themselves and feel able to trust others, this is unlikely to be true of those who compensate for their insecurity in any of the five ways just mentioned:

- Seekers after admiration and applause will do so by misrepresenting reality so as to put themselves in a favourable light.

- Scapegoaters certainly will not have others' well-being at heart, and will have low trust in their followers.

- Distant and self-contained leaders will have their motives questioned, since they give out few indications of what they are thinking or feeling. They will form few relationships, so providing few opportunities for trust to develop.

- Leaders who fear the success of others will be accused of failing to have the organization's best interests as their main concern. Also, because they have low trust in their own abilities, they will fail to inspire trust from others.

- Control freaks will have the lust for power attributed to them (when what they are actually after is security). They fail to trust anyone else, and consequently inspire little trust in themselves.

The conclusion seems to be that some who achieve high positions in organizations may be particularly liable to deal with their insecurity, if they feel any, in ways which are likely to reduce trust.

HOW TO REPAIR TRUST

The previous analysis of the loss of trust and some possible explanations for that loss pave the way for some suggestions as to how it might be repaired. It has often been remarked that trust is only necessary in those situations where it is possible for one party to take advantage of the other.[9] Where such mutual vulnerability has been legislated out, trust is unnecessary. Where it exists, however, a degree of empathy is necessary. We have to understand where the other is feeling vulnerable in order to reassure them that we are not about to take advantage of them. But the fact that we ourselves are vulnerable may make it easier for us to empathize with their insecurity. These considerations, together with our previous analysis, lead to a programme for the renewal of trust, in four stages.

Admission by top management

Top management admits that it has paid insufficient attention in the recent past to employees' diverse needs. It may seek to explain this short-coming in terms of business pressures, but it will nevertheless attribute part of the blame to its own limited perspective.

Limited process of career contracting

Top management engages in a limited process of career contracting as described in Chapter 6. This particular process will be concerned with a specific transition, for example, to part-time shiftwork from full-time for a certain category of workers. Both parties are clearly vulnerable: the organization by committing itself to a process of contracting whereby it promises to take the individual's wants into account; individuals because they are being asked to make a major job transition which may affect their physical or psychological well-being. Both therefore are likely to be risk averse in this initial dealing process. The deal will consequently be a transactional one, with a few elements to the deal, all of them spelt out clearly.

This is a good way of re-establishing trust from a low point, since it offers the opportunity to fulfil the bargain quickly and without ambiguity. Both the process and the outcomes are likely to enhance trust: the process because it exemplifies treating people with dignity and respect and seeking to enhance their welfare; and the outcomes because the management will be seen to have done what it said it would do. There are, however, penalties if things do not work out.[10] If one of the parties violates the deal, the whole project is back to square one. All possible hints of violation must be avoided like the plague, since we can be sure that on this first occasion both parties will be checking up on each other like hawks. Moreover, if either party's needs are not met, the transition will not be successfully made by the business or by individuals. However, these penalties are not dire in their consequences. For the organization, if it is wise, will not have trumpeted from the rooftops its intention to engage in career contracting. It will have saved all that until later, when everything has worked out well a few times.

Establishment of 'knowledge-based' trust

The third step is to establish 'knowledge-based' trust. In other words, trust is beginning to be based not on a specific transactional deal which has penalties attached, but on a developing perception of trustworthiness.[11] Several different career deals may by now have been struck. They are seen to have worked, with both parties having kept their side of the bargain. Moreover, the parties are beginning to feel that each other's behaviour is more predictable. They each seem to have consistent wants and make consistent offers; the dealing process has been similar on each occasion in terms of its four fundamental stages having successfully occurred; the transitions themselves have been successfully negotiated.

Now that trustworthiness has been attributed to the other, then the attributions for the causes of any failures are likely to be more generous.

> They intended to stick to the deal, but they had to drop everything to fight the takeover threat. I'm sure they'll get back to it just as soon as they can.

> The new role's more complex than we originally thought, so he'll obviously need longer to get up to speed.

But such friendly attributions are hard earned – they only occur if there is a history of deals honestly made and honestly kept. And if either party really does welsh on the deal and is perceived to have done so, then the price in lost trustworthiness is greater than at stage 2.

Trust based on identification

This final stage is seldom reached in practice, although human resource management rhetoric supposes that it can be achieved by culture change programmes and the like. It is the achievement of trust on the basis of identification with the other.[12] This form of trust is achieved by each party empathizing with the other's needs and as a consequence taking them on board themselves. In effect the parties become agents for the other's interests. Hence if they share identities, goals and values, this form of trust is more likely, since it is easier to empathize with someone like oneself in these respects. If, however, there is a major gulf between the categories by which the parties define themselves, then empathy becomes next to impossible. It is hard to empathize with someone whom you perceive to be a fat cat when you are relatively speaking a mere mouse.

Top management often seeks to engineer identification with 'the organization', in the belief that its own goal will be seen to be organizational success, and that others will share the same goal.[13] However, top management's previous behaviour may have led to an attribution of more selfish motives. The attempt to suggest that both parties' interests are the same will then fail, and any common identification with the organization be in jeopardy.

Rather, the need is for the parties to seek to **empathize** with the different wants of the other. To imagine a degree of insecurity which threatens the basics of life may be very hard for a top management which has never been in physical need. By the same token, to recognize feelings of uncertainty and insecurity in general may be far easier for both parties. Officers and crew and powder monkeys were all on the same boat together. But again, this perception of common fate is itself a fragile flower, instantly crushed by the realization of the different outcomes that will happen to the parties should the good ship sink.

Perhaps the best hope of empathy is a general human sympathy which transcends organizational position and power inequalities. Identification is not with the organization but with the other. The greatest leaders have always been able to persuade their followers that they were not fundamentally different from them.[14] And many followers can dimly imagine the weight of responsibility borne by their leaders. The leaders and the led can identify with one another at a human level. The CEO of a heavy manufacturing organization can understand the unmanning of the male workforce when heavy manual work disappears. The telesales staff see their manager striving to meet targets ratcheted up yet higher, and imagine the pressure she must be under.

At earlier levels of trust-building, mutuality is a consequence of the career contract. Deals delivering mutual benefits are struck and kept, and the relationship is calculative and instrumental. At the level of identification, however, the calculative motive is not paramount, for each party has the other's interests at heart.[15] As a result, new possibilities emerge for trust to grow further. Trusting behaviour by one of the parties may be seen as sending such messages as 'I value my colleagues' or 'I value an atmosphere of trust', since a calculative attribution is neither necessary nor appropriate.[16] Yet, when trust based on identification is perceived to have been violated, the consequence is likely to be catastrophic. While every effort will be made to attribute the breakdown to other factors, if the other is believed to have lost identification and sympathy, then it is likely to be down the slippery slope to stage 2 again; or rather, to stage 1, since the first step is to apologize for the new violation.

LEADERSHIP: CHARISMATIC OR TACIT?

At least the first three of these stages of trust renewal are, we argue, necessary for organizational and individual transitions to be successfully negotiated. And this is where the exercise of leadership (as opposed to management) becomes paramount. For as we have already remarked, the renewal of trust is a chicken and egg situation. We cannot hope to negotiate transition deals unless the negotiating parties have a modicum of trust in each other. But the fulfilment of agreements made in these self-same deals is apparently the major way in which trust can develop. Leadership of the highest order is required to get the process started. Indeed, the very first step is for top management to be big enough to admit responsibility for the loss of trust. Equal leadership is required from among employees to persuade colleagues to suspend their mistrust and engage in the dealing process with an open mind. And leadership of the HR function is also of the essence in persuading colleagues to undertake a brokering role, on the landing rather than upstairs.

One thing is certain. Top management can rely less and less these days on respect for its position in the hierarchy, as positional power of this sort depends upon a respect for institutions and authority. Social surveys repeatedly demonstrate that such respect has long been on the decrease in the western world. This is not to say, of course, that top management does not retain sufficient positional power to take such actions as acquisitions, mergers, restructuring, or redundancies. Indeed it could be argued that 'managers' right to manage' has seldom been stronger in the second half of the twentieth century than it is at present. Rather, we maintain that respect for and trust in top management because it is top management has decreased.

Charismatic leadership

They therefore have to rely more upon themselves than upon their position if they are to exercise leadership successfully. The question is: what sort of personal power do they need? One recent but at present inappropriate response has been to suggest that they need to be charismatic. Charismatic leaders:[17] [18]

- engage in continuous impression management so as consciously to affect the way people perceive them

- do unconventional things or do things in unconventional ways in order to send messages they want people to hear (on the principle that actions speak louder than words, and symbolic actions speak loudest of all)

- present an appealing and simple vision of what the organization could become, preferably buttressed with some ideological values

- behave in the ways they want others to behave, on the assumption that others will model themselves upon them

- take personal risks on behalf of the organization.

This form of leadership was promoted in the west during the 1980s, when it was realized that organizations faced radical change as a consequence of the changes in the business environment. It was aimed at transforming organizations from one state into another, which, it was believed, was more appropriate to the new realities. Charismatic corporate heroes emerged (Barnevik, Branson, etc.),[19] who delivered the particular organizational transitions deemed necessary at the time (devolution, expansion). Yet our perceptions of the nature of organizational existence have changed in the interim. We construe organizational change in the 1990s as an ongoing series of transitions, not as a single transformation. Hence charismatic leadership is unlikely to work now, even if it did then.

There are other reasons why charismatic leadership is inappropriate today:

- Charismatic leaders tend to possess those personality characteristics which lead all too readily to one of the deformations of power we described earlier.[20] They have a strong need for power, they are highly self-confident and they have very strong convictions. Such individuals only too easily seek admiration and applause and persecute dissenters.

- Employees (and people in general) are far more sophisticated about and resistant to conscious attempts to manipulate them. The presentational elements of all forms of marketing have consequently become very indirect (e.g. humour). Or they concentrate on presenting virtuous actions by the organization which are verifiable and visible.

- Above and beyond this increased sophistication, trust in top management is at a low point in many organizations, so employees will be looking to attribute manipulative motives to their actions.

Tacit leadership

What sort of leadership is appropriate to an era of repeated organizational and individual transitions? First, it is a leadership based on tacit knowledge. What makes knowledge tacit? It is:[21]

- know-how about what to do and when
- also about what not to do and when not to do it
- acquired by experience of what usually results from actions in situations
- seldom, unwillingly and with difficulty verbalized.

What forms of tacit skills are needed by today's organizational leaders, at all levels of the organization? They are:[22]

- Self-knowledge about how to deal with one's motives; in particular, how to cope with the need for power and with insecurity around that power
- Social knowledge about how to deal with others; in particular, the way to:
  - empathize with others and understand their insecurity, need for equity etc.
  - cooperate with others using tact and diplomacy
  - persuade others rationally, consultatively, or by personal or inspirational appeal.

- Organizational knowledge about how to:
  - analyze the current and likely future situation of the organization in its context
  - take different perspectives in so doing
  - nevertheless see the wood for the trees
  - infer and clearly present ways to make the necessary transitions.

Organizational leadership is therefore about having tacit knowledge. It is also about integrity: integrity both in the sense of being integrated as a person, and also in the sense of being trustworthy. One of the many perils of leadership in modern organizations is that of a splitting of the person so that personal and business life occur in separate watertight compartments.[23] The fundamental problem is not therefore one of allowing too little time to one's personal life. It is rather one of failure to incorporate one's personal life into one's business life.

The consequence of failing to do so is the frequently visible imbalance between the three forms of tacit knowledge. Most top managers are excellent at organizational knowledge. Many have acquired well-honed cooperative and persuasive skills. Some are capable of considerable empathy with those in the lower rather than the upper echelons of their organizations. Self-knowledge is another matter, and very hard to assess. Empathy and self-knowledge in particular are more likely to flourish when the personal and the professional lives are integrated, since the personal life can provide a wider variety of sources of knowledge.

The implication for leadership development is that the development of strategic and negotiation skills may be entrusted to the business schools, but the greater needs for empathy and self-knowledge are far more personally recognized and met. What forms might such development take? We should note:

- It is very hard to assess these softer skills as competencies.[24]

- Coaching may enhance interpersonal skills, but these may be perceived as manipulative unless they are underpinned with empathy.

- Empathy is hard to acquire unless one has experienced, or seen at first hand, the life and work of those with whom one has to empathize. Managers with disabled children have an entirely different attitude to disability at the workplace.

- The more top management is selected and groomed from elite institutions, and the greater the difference between the lifestyles of those at the top and bottom of organizations, the harder it is to acquire empathy. Lengthy spells at the sharp end early in their careers are appropriate prescriptions for such elite cadres.

- The greater the insecurity felt by top management as individuals, the less likely they are to open themselves up to this sort of experience.

Enhancing mutual trust so that organizational and individual transitions can be negotiated successfully is the most immediate and important task of the leaders of today's organizations. Fortunately, some at all levels of organizations do have the tacit knowledge and the integrity to achieve it. This is just as well, since leadership has to be exercised by representatives of both parties to the deal. Both parties have to be led to take an initial step of faith, and both have to deal in good faith. Both parties also have to be led to keep the deals they make, whatever short-term gains they may forgo by so doing. And both have to be led to take a broad contextual view of the arena in which they are doing deals. Then, with trust restored, organizations can face their uncertain future with a good chance of at least changing quickly enough to survive and even prosper.

Joshua Slocum has to have the last word, of course, since we can be sure that he would have negotiated his passage through organizational transitions with the same ingenuity and skill that he negotiated the oceans:

> To face the elements is, to be sure, no light matter when the sea is in its grandest mood. You must then know the sea, and know that you know it, and not forget that it was made to be sailed over.

Some questions to think about

1. Think of some controversial actions by top management in your organization. To what did employees attribute these actions? To the business situation? To various motives? To ability or lack of it? Why, in your judgement, did they make the attributions that they did?

2. Can you recall an instance when parties in your organization admitted that they had made a mistake and apologized? Why did they do so? Were they forced into it, or did they do it voluntarily? What were the consequences?

3. Can you recall an occasion when one or the other party went the extra mile for the other? Why do you think this happened?

4. Does your organization engage in any activities aimed at developing leadership skills? What forms do these activities take, and what leadership skills in particular are they aimed at? Who participates, and how if at all is the success of the activities assessed?

REFERENCES

1 Mishra, A.K. (1996) 'Organizational responses to crisis', in R.M. Kramer and T. R. Tyler (eds) *Trust in Organizations: Frontiers of Theory and Research*. Thousand Oaks, CA: Sage.

2 Tyler, T.R. and Degoey, P. (1996) 'Trust in organizational authorities: the influence of motive attributions on willingness to accept decisions', in R.M. Kramer and T.R.Tyler (eds) *Trust in Organizations: Frontiers of Theory and Research*. Thousand Oaks, CA: Sage.

3 Tyler, T.R. and Bies, R.J. (1990) 'Interpersonal aspects of procedural justice', in J.S. Carroll (ed.) *Applied Social Psychology in Business Settings*. Hillsdale, NJ: Lawrence Erlbaum.

4 *The Guardian*, 11 July 1997.
5 The *Observer*, 13 July 1997.
6 Hutton, W. (1994) *The State We're In*. London: Jonathan Cape.
7 Kets de Vries, M.F.R. (1994) 'The leadership mystique'. *Academy of Management Executive* 8 (3): 73–89.
8 Kets de Vries, M.F.R. (1993) *Leaders, Fools, and Impostors*. San Francisco: Jossey Bass.
9 Deutsch, M. (1973) *The Resolution of Conflict: Constructive and Destructive Processes*. New Haven, CT: Yale University Press.
10 Axelrod, R. (1984) *The Evolution of Cooperation*. New York: Basic Books.
11 Rotter, J.B. (1971) 'Generalized expectancies for interpersonal trust'. *American Psychologist* 26: 443–52.
12 Kramer, R.M. (1993) 'Cooperation and organizational identification', in K.Murnighan (ed.) *Social Psychology in Organizations: Advances in Theory and Research*. Englewood Cliffs, NJ: Prentice-Hall.
13 Coopey, J. and Hartley, J. (1991) 'Reconsidering the case for organisational commitment'. *Human Resource Management Journal* 1 (3): 18–32.
14 Gardner, H. (1996) *An Anatomy of Leadership*. London: HarperCollins.
15 Barber, B. (1983) *The Logic and Limits of Trust*. New Brunswick, NJ: Rutgers University Press.
16 Kramer, R.M., Brewer, M.B. and Hanna, B.A. (1996) 'Collective trust and collective action: the decision to trust as a social decision', in R.M. Kramer and T.R. Tyler (eds) *Trust in Organizations: Frontiers of Theory and Research*. Thousand Oaks, CA: Sage.
17 House, R.J. (1977) 'A theory of charismatic leadership', in J.G. Hunt and L.L. Larson (eds) *Leadership: The Cutting Edge*. Carbondale, IL: Southern Illinois University Press.
18 Conger, J.A. and Kanungo, R. (1987) 'Toward a behavioural theory of charismatic leadership in organisational settings'. *Academy of Management Review* 12: 637–47.
19 Kets de Vries, M.F.R. (1996) 'Leaders who make a difference'. *European Management Journal* 14 (5): 486–93.
20 Conger, J.A. (1989) *The Charismatic Leader: Behind the Mystique of Exceptional Leadership*. San Francisco: Jossey Bass.
21 Polanyi, M. (1976) 'Tacit knowledge', in M. Marx and F. Goodson (eds) *Theories in Contemporary Psychology*. New York: Macmillan.
22 Sternberg, R.J. (1997) 'Tacit knowledge and job success', in N. Anderson and P. Herriot (eds) *International Handbook of Selection and Assessment*. Chichester: Wiley.
23 Scase, R. and Goffee, R. (1989) *Reluctant Managers: Their Work and Lifestyles*. London: Unwin Hyman.
24 Strebler, M., Robinson, D. and Heron, P. (1997) 'Getting the best out of your competencies'. Brighton: Institute for Employment Studies, Report 334.

Epilogue

Slocum's epic voyage was a lonely one. Many of the top people in organizations today feel equally lonely. While a multitude of different stakeholders make their expectations of them only too obvious, they themselves have few in whom they feel they can confide. Where they do find kindred spirits, these are often people from their own background with whom they can rapidly identify on the basis of shared experiences of business and organizational change.

But many employees also feel isolated and insecure in the turmoil of transition. The sources of their insecurity may be very different from that of their bosses, but the feelings are similar. Insecurity in both is potentially destructive to the organization. Top people's insecurity can manifest itself in a variety of organizationally lethal defensive behaviours. Employee insecurity may be more insidious in its effects, but in time it is just as destructive.

The first message of this book is that career transitions are the very central pillar of organizational survival. Organizational transitions are necessary to keep the ship on course in stormy business seas; and for organizational transitions to occur, individual career transitions have to occur also.

The second message is that transition and trust are inextricably intertwined. Employees will only make the journey if they trust top management and if top management trusts them. To break the vicious circle of mistrust and imposed change, career contracting has to happen, for career contracting facilitates transitions and enhances trust.

The third and final message is that we have to stop talking about such areas as career management as though they are purely technical issues to be addressed by knowledgeable and skilled professionals and solved by systems. Emotions of the most profound nature are involved here. Only when we recognize them in ourselves and others and act accordingly will we progress the debate and affect outcomes.

However, this is not a 'touchy feely' book, although we happen to believe that emotions are underplayed in discussions of organizations.

Rather, it is about the necessary conditions for organizational survival. All sorts of unlikely people are coming to realize that companies' futures lie in the hands of their employees. What we have done is to point to the re-establishment of trust as the fundamental element in negotiating the transitions ahead.

So this is a business book after all, for it is about the conditions for the success or failure of businesses.

Index

adjustment 65, 68, 118–20
affect 112, 120–7, 140–1
age and work 12, 54
agency, 5, 122
Alcoholics Anonymous 123
America 18, 83
anticipatory socialization 117, 140
Argyris, C. 111
Asea Brown Boveri (ABB) 73
Atkinson, J. 6
attribution 57, 165–8, 171
Australia 49

Barnevik, P. 174
Bass 136, 154
behaviour, rational vs affective 27–8,
    120–7, 140–1
board membership 141–2
Branson, R. 174
Bridges, W. 12
British Airways (BA) 116
British American Tobacco (BAT) 79
British Petroleum (BP) 23, 133
British Telecommunications (BT) 34,
    77
business
    information 133–4
    priorities 167–8
    process reengineering 36–7

Cable & Wireless 116
Canada 49
career
    anchors 96–9, 114, 153
    as transition 66–8, 71

contracting 100–106, 129–44,
    155–60, 170
    management 7, 84, 147–61
    questionnaires 137–9
    resilience 114–15
    workshops 135–7
cataclysm 12–14, 73–4
Catalonia 20
centralization vs devolution 81–2,
    130–1, 149–50
charismatic leadership 173–4
China 14, 18, 19
City of London 40, 66
Civil Service 82
collectivism 23–4, 123–6
commitment 6
common fate 41
competencies 133–4
competition 27–8
Connor, H. 33
continuity 11–12, 73–5
contract
    and HR processes 101–2
    and information 143
    career 96–102, 129–44, 155–60, 170
    elements of 156–60
    management of 94–5, 155–60
    process 101–102
    psychological 21–2, 124
    social 21–2, 52
    stages of 155–60
cost
    competitiveness 5, 29
    cutting 29–31, 33
credibility 41–2

crime 53, 55
culture 19, 39, 40–1, 83

Denmark 49
Department for Education and
   Employment (DfEE) 134
development 109–12, 115–7, 126–7
   of leadership 176–7
development centres 136
dilemmas
   centralization vs devolution 81–2
   cost competitiveness vs innovation
      5, 29–31, 78, 94
   growth vs contraction 78
   long vs short termism 79–80
downsizing 34–5, 50–1, 125–6, 159–60

economic change 14–17
economists 11–13
empathy 169, 172–3, 176
employability 97
employee
   assistance programmes 159
   wants and offers 134–7
encounter 65, 68, 117
equity 43, 154, 158–9
   procedural 166
European Union (EU) 37, 41

family 52–3, 176
finance sector 40, 64, 124
First Direct 124
flexibility 6–7, 28–9, 35–6, 97–99, 101,
   151, 153
Ford 109
Fukuyama, F., 18
fundamentalism 20

Galbraith, J. K. 19
gender 50, 54–5, 124
Germany 18
globalization 14–17
government 19
graduates 33, 70, 82, 84
Grand Metropolitan 79
Gratton, L. 57

growth vs contraction 77–8, 130,
   149–50

Hamel, G. 4
Hampden-Turner, C. 74
Handy, C. 36, 51, 75
Hanson 79
Hewlett–Packard 134
Hong Kong 20
hours of work 37
human resource
   function 28–9, 31, 39, 81, 115
   processes 100–2, 143–4, 147–9,
      160–1
   rhetoric 40
   strategy 62–3, 73–4, 78–80

ICL 154
identification 171–2
identity 53–6, 96, 121
Imperial Chemical Industries (ICI) 79
implementation (of the contract)
   155–6
India 15
individualism 22–3
information
   and career contracting 129–44
   and trust 138, 144
information technology 15
innovation 5, 29–31, 78
inplacement 95–6
insecurity 11–12, 48–53
Institute of Management 52
institutions 21, 52–3
International Business Machines
   (IBM) 94, 99
Investors in People 134
issuism 20
Italy 18

Japan 18, 83
John Lewis 151
just-in-time management 84, 150–1

knowledge
   based trust 170–1

knowledge *continued*
   tacit 175–7
   work 54
Korea 83

labour market power 157
leadership 163–77
   and personality 167–9
   and trust 164
   charismatic 173–4
   development of 176–7
   tacit 175–7
learning 109–12
   barriers to 111
   double loop 111
   from transitions 115–17, 125
line management 81
Lloyds TSB 124
Lombardia 20
long vs short termism 78–80, 130,
   149–50

McDonald's 48
management
   just-in-time 84, 150–1
   line 81
   of affect 123–6
   of contracting 94–5, 155–60
   of transitions 65–6, 115–17, 147–61
   tools 28
manufacturing 124
Marks and Spencer 23, 80, 83, 151
Mintzberg, H. 39
mistrust 41–3, 58, 166–7
Mobil 23
monitoring the contract 157–9

National Health Service (NHS) 19, 21
nationalism 20
NatWest 99
negotiation of contract 156–7
New Zealand 21
Nicholson, N. 65
Norway 49

on the job training 118–19

organization
   citizenship 23
   offers 137–9
   size 54–5
   socialization within 119–20
   strategy 27–8, 30–1, 61–3
   structure 62
   tenure 35, 50
   transitions 65–6, 73–85
   wants 130–4
outsourcing 36

part-time work 50–1
Pascale, R. 74
pensions 52
perceptions 13–14
performance-related pay 32
personality 167–9
Peters, T. 12
pharmaceutical 69–70, 136
Pitcher, J. 33
Pollard, E. 33
Post Office 134
poverty 21, 53
Prahalad, C.K. 4
preparation for transition 65, 68, 117
Price Waterhouse 80
procedural equity 166
productivity 36–7
professionalism 20
psychological contract 21–2, 124
public vs private sector 55
Purcell, K. 33

realistic previews 140
reciprocity 23, 42–3
redundancy 34–5, 49–51, 125–6,
   159–60
reflection 111
regionalism 20
renegotiation 159–60
resilience 114–5
rhetoric 37–41, 56–7, 101
Rolls-Royce 53
Rover 96, 109, 151

Schein, E. 97
security 47–9, 51–2, 99
self-esteem 121–2, 168–9
segmentation 33–4, 104, 151, 154–5
Shell 12, 77, 95, 134
Shenzhen 20
Slocum, J. 3–4, 8, 48–9, 56, 62–3, 76,
    97, 114, 129, 177
social capital 8, 17–21, 27, 43–4
    change 18–19
    contract 21–2, 52
    issues 14
splitting 125, 175–6
stabilization 65, 68
strategy 27–8, 30–3, 61–3
    emergent 39, 61
    HR 62–3, 73–4, 78–80
succession planning 133
Sun Microsystems 135

tacit leadership 175–7
tenure 35, 50
top management 57–8, 163–77
    personality of 168–9
total quality management 32–3
Toyota 73
trade unions 51
training and development 33–4,
    125–7
transaction costs 18, 44
transformation 12–14
transition
    affect in 112
    and career anchors 96–9

career as 66–7
consequences of 94, 95–9
development for 109–27
frequency of 83
learning from 115–7
management of 65–6, 115–7, 143–51
organizational 65–6, 73–85
phases of 65–6, 68–70, 115–21,
    147–9
preparation for 65, 68, 117
process of 63–5, 113
trends 11–12, 54–5, 73–5
trust
    and collectivism 23–4
    and information 138, 144
    and security 47–9
    identification-based 171–2
    knowledge-based 170–1
    nature of 42–3, 164–5
    restoration of 56–8, 97–8, 169–72

unemployment 49–50
Unilever 83
unitarist vs pluralist 153, 172
United Kingdom (UK) 12, 13, 15, 17,
    21–2, 32, 36–7, 49, 53, 98, 159
United States (USA) 22–3, 49, 55, 159
up to speed 118

Vauxhall 109–10
Vickers 119

Weick, K. 39, 62
West, M.A. 65
WH Smith 81